SpringerBriefs in Computer Science

SpringerBriefs present concise summaries of cutting-edge research and practical applications across a wide spectrum of fields. Featuring compact volumes of 50 to 125 pages, the series covers a range of content from professional to academic.

Typical topics might include:

- A timely report of state-of-the art analytical techniques
- A bridge between new research results, as published in journal articles, and a contextual literature review
- A snapshot of a hot or emerging topic
- An in-depth case study or clinical example
- A presentation of core concepts that students must understand in order to make independent contributions

Briefs allow authors to present their ideas and readers to absorb them with minimal time investment. Briefs will be published as part of Springer's eBook collection, with millions of users worldwide. In addition, Briefs will be available for individual print and electronic purchase. Briefs are characterized by fast, global electronic dissemination, standard publishing contracts, easy-to-use manuscript preparation and formatting guidelines, and expedited production schedules. We aim for publication 8–12 weeks after acceptance. Both solicited and unsolicited manuscripts are considered for publication in this series.

More information about this series at http://www.springer.com/series/10028

Santosh Singh Rathore · Sandeep Kumar

Fault Prediction Modeling for the Prediction of Number of Software Faults

Santosh Singh Rathore
Department of Computer Science and
Engineering
ABV-Indian Institute of Information
Technology and Management Gwalior
Gwalior, Madhya Pradesh, India

Sandeep Kumar
Department of Computer Science and
Engineering
Indian Institute of Technology Roorkee
Roorkee, Uttarakhand, India

ISSN 2191-5768   ISSN 2191-5776   (electronic)
SpringerBriefs in Computer Science
ISBN 978-981-13-7130-1   ISBN 978-981-13-7131-8   (eBook)
https://doi.org/10.1007/978-981-13-7131-8

Library of Congress Control Number: 2019934353

This Springer imprint is published by the registered company Springer Nature Singapore Pte Ltd.
The registered company address is: 152 Beach Road, #21-01/04 Gateway East, Singapore 189721,
Singapore

Preface

Software fault prediction (SFP) can be defined as a process of predicting the fault-proneness of the given software modules using some historic software fault data. For the given software, SFP predicts faulty modules via the use of various software metrics and the fault information collected from the software repositories. The main aim of SFP is to reduce the fault-finding efforts and to increase the quality of the software. To help the software testers and managers, SFP process attempts to provide useful hints by identifying the probable faulty code areas that require extensive testing or refactoring. The typical software fault prediction model is constructed by using some machine learning or statistical techniques and is used to predict software module being faulty on non-faulty. Another way to predict the fault-proneness of the software modules is by predicting number of faults in a module.

In this book, we focus on the prediction of number of faults in the software modules. First, we discuss the generalized process of the software fault prediction and classification of software faults. Next, we discuss various regression techniques and ensemble methods for the prediction of number of faults. Subsequently, we discuss the state-of-the-art literature focusing on the prediction of number of faults. Further, we evaluate different techniques and some ensemble methods for the prediction of number of faults.

This book is organized into six chapters. Chapter 1 introduces the concept of software fault prediction and prediction of the number of faults. The chapter also discusses various classification schemes of software faults and provides information about the contribution and organization of this book. Chapter 2 provides a description of different regression techniques used for the prediction of number of faults. In addition, the chapter also provides a description of the ensemble methods and summarized the state-of-the-art techniques used for the prediction of number of faults in software systems. Chapter 3 presents an experimental analysis of homogeneous ensemble methods for the prediction of number of faults including details of used software fault datasets and categorization of fault datasets into different groups. Chapter 4 presents an experimental study of linear rule-based ensemble methods for the prediction of number of faults and discusses the results. Chapter 5 presents an experimental study of non-linear rule-based ensemble methods for the prediction of number of faults and discusses the results. Chapter 6 concludes this book.

Gwalior, India   Santosh Singh Rathore
Roorkee, India   Sandeep Kumar

Acknowledgements

First, I would like to extend my sincere gratitude to Almighty God. I would like to express my sincere thanks to my institute, ABV-Indian Institute of Information Technology and Management Gwalior, India, for providing me a healthy and conducive working environment. I would also like to extend my thanks to National Institute of Technology, Jalandhar for providing me all necessary supports. I also express my thanks to the many people who provided their support in writing this book, either directly or indirectly. I thank Dr. Sandeep Kumar for the impetus to write this book. I want to acknowledge my sisters and parents for their blessing and persistent backing. I thank all my friends and colleagues for being a source of inspiration and love throughout my journey. I want to thank anonymous reviewers for proofreading the chapters and the publishing team.

—Santosh Singh Rathore

I would like to express my sincere thanks to my institute, Indian Institute of Technology Roorkee, India, for providing me a healthy and conducive working environment. I am also thankful to the faculty members of the Department of Computer Science and Engineering, Indian Institute of Technology Roorkee, India, for their constant support and encouragement. I am especially thankful to some of my colleagues, who are more like friends and give me constant support. I am grateful to the editor and the publication team of Springer for their constant cooperation in writing this book. I am really thankful to my wife, sisters, brother, parents-in-law, and my lovely daughter Aastha who is my life for their love and blessings. I have no words to mention the love, blessings, support, patience, and sacrifice of my parents. I dedicate this book to God and to my family.

—Sandeep Kumar

Contents

About the Authors

Dr. Santosh Singh Rathore is currently working as an Assistant Professor at ABV-Indian Institute of Information Technology and Management (IIITM), Gwalior, India. Earlier, he has worked as an Assistant Professor at National Institute of Technology Jalandhar. He has received M.Tech. from the Indian Institute of Information Technology Design and Manufacturing (IIITDM) Jabalpur, India, and Ph.D. from the Indian Institute of Technology Roorkee, Roorkee, India. He has published research papers in various referred journals and national and international conferences. Also, he has published a book in the SpringerBrief in Computer Science. His research interests include software fault prediction, software quality assurance, empirical software engineering, object-oriented software development, object-oriented metrics, and application of soft computing in software engineering. Email: santosh.srathore@gmail.com.

Dr. Sandeep Kumar (SMIEEE'17) is currently working as an Associate Professor in the Department of Computer Science and Engineering at the Indian Institute of Technology (IIT) Roorkee, India. He has supervised three Ph.D. theses, about 40 master dissertations, about 15 undergraduate projects, and is currently supervising five Ph.D. students. He has published more than 60 research papers in international/national journals and conferences and has also written books/book-chapters with Springer (USA) and IGI Publications (USA). He has also filed two patents for his work done along with his students. Dr. Sandeep is the member of the board of examiners and board of studies of various universities and institutions. He has collaborations in industry and academia. He is currently handling multiple national and international research/consultancy projects. He has received Young Faculty Research Fellowship award from MeitY (Govt. of India), NSF/TCPP early adopter award-2014, 2015, ITS Travel Award 2011 and 2013, and others. He is a member of ACM and senior member of IEEE. His name has also been enlisted in major directories such as Marquis Whos Who, IBC, and others. His areas of interest include Semantic Web, Web Services, and Software Engineering. Email: sandeepkumargarg@gmail.com, sgargfec@iitr.ac.in

Chapter 1
Introduction

In today's world, software is the key element for the functionality of almost all engineered and automated systems. Due to this evolution, reliability and quality of software systems become crucial for the successful functioning of day-to-day operations. Fault-proneness of the software components has a direct impact on the quality and reliability of the software system. A higher number of faults generally signifies poor software quality and low software reliability. Generally, software testing is performed to detect and fix faults in the software components. However, testing resources are usually limited and therefore a thorough and cavernous testing is not possible. Software fault prediction, which aims to predict risky code areas in the software system, can assist the testing process by raising alarms for such code areas and can help developers in detecting faults and optimizing their testing efforts. With the aim to provide the basic understanding of software fault prediction, this chapter discusses the fundamentals of software faults, software fault prediction process, and advantages of software fault prediction in the software development life cycle.

1.1 Software Fault Prediction

Software testing is tedious, resource consuming but important process in the software development lifecycle. Ideally, a large portion of software development resources is allotted to the software testing and software quality assurances activities [1]. Modern-day software systems are growing complex and larger in size, thus making the task of software testing and quality assurance more difficult. The ultimate goal of the software testing process is to deliver the software system that is free from any bug and meeting the requirements of the stakeholders. However, ensuring that a software system is free from all faults is required an exhaustive and thorough testing, which is an expensive, almost impossible goal to achieve [11]. In real-world software projects, typically, a small amount of budget is left for the testing. This imposes the need

© The Author(s), under exclusive license to Springer Nature Singapore Pte Ltd. 2019
S. S. Rathore and S. Kumar, *Fault Prediction Modeling for the Prediction of Number of Software Faults*, SpringerBriefs in Computer Science,
https://doi.org/10.1007/978-981-13-7131-8_1

for a prediction model that can guide the software testing process by predicting the risky areas of the code where faults are more likely to occur. This prediction of fault-prone areas of code can result in a more focused testing process and can reduce the overall testing budget and efforts and thus improving the software quality and reliability [16]. The working of software fault prediction (SFP) is based on this underlying requirement. SFP uses the structural and/or development process related characteristics of a software system to make the prediction about fault-prone software components/modules and raise the alarm for these components to prevent faults from propagating in other parts of the software [2]. In this way, SFP helps in streaming software quality assurance efforts and in optimizing the software testing process by testing fault-prone modules first, refactoring the code, etc. [5, 6]. Project managers and developers can use SFP to measure the intermediate quality of the software during development phases and make decisions accordingly to improve the efficiency and quality of the development process [8, 15]. The advantage of quick and timely prediction of faults and to ease the overall software quality assurance process has attracted the noticeable attention of the research community to the software fault prediction.

The working of software fault prediction is founded on the assumption that if a previously developed software component was found faulty under certain environmental conditions, then any component currently under development with similar environmental conditions and with similar structural properties will end to be fault-prone [11]. Thus, the working of SFP is based on the historic fault data stored in the software repositories [18]. Figure 1.1 illustrates the working of software fault prediction. It mainly consists of four different steps [8, 12]:

(1) *Mining of software repository and extraction of data*: A large amount of process-related data has been generated during the development of the software system. This data is stored in the software repositories in terms of log files, source code files, bug repositories, etc. However, this data usually is in the unstructured form and required mining. Collection of software fault dataset requires the mining of this historical data from the repositories. Software fault related information is collected from the bug data repository and the structural- and process-related information is collected from other repositories.

(2) *Extraction of software metric information*: The extracted structural and process related information is transformed into the software metrics. Each software metric is corresponding to one property of the software system. A typical fault dataset contains a set of such metrics. By combining fault's information and extracted software metrics, a fault dataset is created that is used to build and validate the prediction model.

(3) *Building of fault prediction model*: Building of a fault prediction model consists use of learning technique(s) over the fault dataset. Fault dataset is divided into two parts, training dataset, and testing dataset. Training dataset is used to train the learning technique and the testing dataset is used to validate the model. Generally, machine learning or statistical techniques are used as learning techniques in model building.

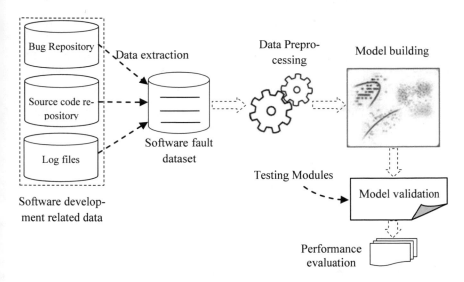

Fig. 1.1 Software fault prediction process

(4) *Assessment of prediction model*: This step consists validation of built prediction model for the unseen testing dataset. Once the training of the prediction model is completed, it is supplied with the testing dataset and the prediction results are recorded. These prediction results are then assessed with respect to the ground truth values (actual class label). Different performance measures are used to evaluate the performance of the prediction model. Once the prediction model passes the threshold performance criteria, it is further used to predict faults in the current and future releases of the software system.

1.2 Classification of Software Faults

In the software development process, a software fault refers to the mismatch between expected and actual output. It is also known as bug or defect. According to IEEE standards, a fault is "an incorrect step, instruction or data in a program" [9]. These faults eventually lead software system to the failure or sometimes may change the external behavior of the program. Black box testing detects functional-level faults and white box testing detects code-level faults. We include both types of faults in the software fault dataset. There many classifications of software faults are available based on their occurrence in the software development life cycle. Knowing the type of fault predicted by the model can leverage the tester in the selection of appropriate measures to locate and fix it. In this subsection, we discuss some of the classifications of faults available in the literature.

Orthogonal defect/fault classification (ODC) scheme has classified software defects into eight different categories [4]. The classification scheme is based on the semantics of defects. It means that a type of defects points to the part of the process that needs attention. The following classes of defects were proposed in this classification. Ning et al. have provided a complete list of ODC defects [13].

1. Function: It refers to the defect that affects end-user functionality such as an interface with hardware, interface with application program, etc., significantly.
2. Assignment: It refers to the defect that occurs in the few lines of code such as initialization of code or data structure.
3. Interface: It refers to the defect that occurs in the interface, which interacts with other components such as modules, device driver, etc.
4. Checking: It refers to the defect that occurs in the program logic, which fails to validate data and values, loop initial, and termination conditions, etc.
5. Timing/serialization: It refers to the defects occurs in the shared resources and global values.
6. Build/package/merge: It refers to the defect occurs due to the errors in library functions and packages.
7. Documentation: It refers to the defect occurs in the documentation and maintenance files.
8. Algorithm: It refers to the defects occurs due to the problem in the algorithm correctness and efficiency.

Another fault classification scheme is based on the severity level of faults [21]. The severity of a fault is defined as the effect of a fault in the failure of the system. It is a subjective measure and varies with the different software systems and with different organizations. A generic category of these faults is given as follows:

1. Show Stopper: It is the most sever category of faults. If a detected fault stops the working of the system, then is classified as show stopper fault. We need to fix this fault before continuing with the testing.
2. Critical: These faults cause serious performance problems such as lose functionality, security concerns, etc., in the system, but do not hamper the testing process. We need to fix these faults before the release of application.
3. Major: These faults cause major problem such as loss of data in the system. These faults do not interrupt the continuance of the testing process.
4. Medium: These faults cause minor performance problems in the system such as deviation from the actual output, displaying wrong data format, etc.
5. Minor: These faults show little or no deviation from the functional requirements.
6. Cosmetic: These faults do not affect the performance of the system, but give slightly different interpretation of output. For instance, issues like fonts, colors, or pitch size, etc., are the types of these faults.

Another category of faults can be based on the occurrence of faults in the code base or during coding. These faults may directly or indirectly manifest themselves into the code. A classification of these faults is given as follows [20].

1. Faults due to pointers and memory: These faults occur in the system due to the mishandling of pointers and due to the memory leaks. Common types of faults in this category are "temporary value returned", "memory leak", "free the already freed resources", "null dereferencing", "exposure of private data to untrusted components", etc.
2. Faults due to aliases: These faults occur due to unexpected aliasing of parameters, return values, and global variables, etc. Common type of fault in this category is "need of unique address", which violated when we expect different addresses.
3. Faults due to synchronization: These faults occur due to the sharing of resources among many threads, which causes synchronization problem. Common types of faults in this category are "deadlocks", "race condition", "live lock", etc.
4. Faults due to data and arithmetic operations: These faults occur due to wrong arithmetic and logical operations. Some common faults in this category are "uninitialized memory", "value outside domain", "buffer overflow/underflow", "arithmetic exceptions", "wrong assumptions of operator precedence", "string handling errors", etc.
5. Faults due to security vulnerabilities: These faults occur due to the use of unsecure operations in the code or due to executing malicious code. Some common faults in this category are "buffer overflow", "gaining root privileges", "exploiting heap overflows", "dealing with volatile objects", etc.
6. Faults due to redundant operations: These faults occur due to redundancies prevail in the program. Common types of faults in this category are "redundant assignment", "dead code", and "redundant conditions".
7. Faults due to inheritance operations: These faults occur due to mishandling of inheritance operation in the code. "Virtual function is not overridden", "component of derived class shadow base class", "override both equal and hashcode" are some common faults found in this category.
8. Other code-related bugs: Some other faults can also occur in the code due to not using coding standard, programmer inexperience, etc. This includes the faults such as "loss of data due to truncate", "comparison of strings as objects", "array index value", etc.

Grottke and Trivedi proposed a classification scheme of software faults [7]. The proposed scheme contains four different categories of faults, which are as follows:

1. Bohrbugs: The faults, which are easy to detect and easy to fix in the software system fall under this category. These faults easily isolate and manifest themselves under a well-defined set of conditions.
2. Mandlebugs: The faults, which are complex in nature fall under this category. The underlying causes of these faults are obscure that make their behavior chaotic and nondeterministic. It is very hard to detect and fix these faults.

Each software fault is either a Bohrbugs or a Mandlebugs.

3. Heisenbugs: This type of faults do not directly cause system failure or affect the system performance. However, they manifest themselves differently when one attempts to probe or isolate them. It is a sub-type of Mandelbug.

4. Aging-related bugs: This type of faults is accumulated in the system due to its long run or due to the system environmental conditions. These faults degrade the system performance over the period of time.

Spiros Mancoridis at Drexel university proposed a classification scheme of faults based on the occurrence in the software development life cycle [19]. The author discusses the following categories of faults. The author used the term bug in the classification scheme, which refers to fault/defect in the software system.

1. Requirement specification bugs: These bugs occur in the requirement specification document due to incomplete, ambiguous, and inconsistent requirements. It is difficult to detect and fix these bugs.
2. Structural bugs: These bugs occur during the design phase of software development. Common bugs in this category are control and sequence bugs, logical bugs, processing bugs, data flow bug, etc. These bugs can be avoided by using good programming practices and modern-day software development standards.
3. Data bugs: These bugs occur from the specification of data entities and their format. These bugs are often difficult to catch.
4. Implementation and coding bugs: These bugs occur due to coding mistakes, misunderstanding of operations, and typological errors during the implementation of software system.
5. Integration bugs: These bugs occur when a software component interfaces with other components and mismatching between interfacing parts. They could be internal interface bugs, external interface bugs, or integration bugs.
6. System and architecture bugs: These bugs occur due to system load, and their symptoms emerge only when the system is stressed. These bugs are very difficult to detect and fix.
7. Testing bugs: These bugs occur due to incorrect execution of test cases or incorrectly written test code.

Additionally, the author reported the frequency of the bugs in each phase of software development. The author has reported the following frequency of bugs.

- Requirements bugs: 24.3%
- Structural bugs: 25.2%
- Data bugs: 22.4%
- Implementation and coding bugs: 9.9%
- Interface bugs: 9.0%
- System and architecture bugs: 1.7%
- Testing bugs: 2.8%

1.3   Advantages of Software Fault Prediction

Software fault prediction is the key in improving the quality of the software system while optimizing the resource utilization and reducing the testing cost. Results of software fault prediction model allow the managers to make the decision about the allocation of development resources effectively and efficiently. Following are some advantages of software fault prediction in the development of software systems:

1. *Reduction in testing efforts*: Software testing consumes the biggest chunk of software development resources. In real-world projects, enough resources are not available to allot to the software testing. Software fault prediction (SFP) plays a crucial role in this situation. Early studies showed that SFP helps in reduction of testing efforts by a great amount. According to the study reported by Monden et al. [17], SFP can reduce total testing cost by 25%. However, authors reported that about 6% of the additional cost inures to the organization in terms of the collection of software metrics, preprocessing dataset, and building fault prediction model when using SFP along with software testing. Therefore, a total of 19% of testing efforts could be saved. In another study, Hryszko and Madeyski [10] showed that quality assurance cost has reduced by 30% when software defect prediction is used along with software testing. Additionally, the authors showed that the presented tool DePress has a return on investment of 73% and the benefit–cost ration of 74%. Moreover, authors deployed the tool to continue usage to the industrial projects run by Volvo group.

2. *Early detection of faults and optimal allocation of resources*: The primary aim of software fault prediction is to help the developer or software tester to identify risky areas of the software system to streamline their testing efforts. Boehm and Papaccio [3] found that removal of faults at design level is cost 50–200 times less costly than removal of faults after the deployment. A study conducted by NASA showed that a fault introduced in the requirement phase, if not removed and leaked into the later phases results in the much higher correction cost [3]. The earlier studies showed that modules ranked as fault-prone by the software fault prediction model used by testers to detect additional faults in the modules that were considered previously to be a low fault-prone. Additionally, modules identified by testers as the most fault-prone are among the top four fault-prone modules identified by the software prediction model. In one of the study, Boehm's highlighted the importance of software fault prediction by showing that the verification effort saved by fault prediction model of correct identification of one fault is higher than the cost of misclassification of a hundred fault-free modules as fault-prone.

3. *Improvement in the reliability of software systems*: Nowadays, software is the key element of function in many modern engineered systems. In this growing number of applications of software, one vital challenge is to ensure the safety or the reliability of the software, i.e., the probability of failure-free operation for the specified period of time in the given environmental conditions. The reliability of the software depends on the software faults. More the faults, lessen the reliability of the software [14]. Many modern-day software engineering practices test the software under specified environment to ensure that software is correct or fault-free. However, it is an expensive and time-consuming process to test the whole system thoroughly due to the increasing size and complexity of the software. One of the potential solutions to this problem is to bring together two reasonings,

about evidence of correctness (software testing) and about the probability of certain faults (software fault prediction) that can lead to the failure. Software fault prediction addresses this issue to develop more reliable software systems, thus strengthen the safety of the software.

1.4   Organization of the Book

Chapter 2 discusses different techniques used for the prediction of number of faults in software systems. It includes the discussion of regression techniques and ensemble methods. Further, the state-of-the-art of these techniques for the prediction of number of faults is presented. Additionally, details of used performance evaluation measures are provided.

Chapter 3 presents details of homogeneous ensemble methods for software fault prediction. Further, the chapter presents an evaluation of these methods for the prediction of number of faults in software systems. The chapter also provides details of the used software fault datasets, experimental procedure, and performance evaluation measures.

Chapter 4 presents linear rule based heterogeneous ensemble methods for software fault prediction. Further, the chapter presents an experimental evaluation of these methods for the prediction of number of faults in software systems. Description of used software fault datasets, experimental procedure is also presented. Results of the analysis are discussed at the end of the chapter.

Chapter 5 discusses nonlinear rule-based heterogeneous ensemble methods for software fault prediction. Further, the chapter presents an experimental evaluation of these methods for the prediction of number of faults in software systems. Description of used software fault datasets, experimental procedure is also presented. Results of the analysis are discussed at the end of the chapter.

Chapter 6 concludes the book by summarizing the topics discussed in the book.

1.5   Summary

In the past few decades, software fault prediction has been one of the most active areas of software engineering research. It makes use of software structural- and product-related metrics augmented with fault information to infer useful patterns and rules to predict fault occurrences or risky code areas in future software releases. This quality of software fault prediction can help developers to build software components having a lesser number of faults effectively and help managers to meet quality goals of under developing software in a cost-effective manner. This chapter introduced fundamental concepts of the software fault prediction. Basics terminologies of software fault prediction, classification of software faults/bugs, and benefits of software fault prediction have also been discussed. In the end, chapter summarized the organization of the book.

References

1. Adrion, W.R., Branstad, M.A., Cherniavsky, J.C.: Validation, verification, and testing of computer software. ACM Comput. Surv. **14**(2), 159–192 (1982)
2. Arisholm, E., Briand, L., Johannessen, E.B.: A systematic and comprehensive investigation of methods to build and evaluate fault prediction models. J. Syst. Softw. **83**(1), 2–17 (2010)
3. Boehm, B.W., Papaccio, P.N.: Understanding and controlling software costs. IEEE Trans. Softw. Eng. **14**(10), 1462–1477 (1988)
4. Bridge, N., Miller, C.: Orthogonal defect classification using defect data to improve software development. Softw. Qual. **3**(1), 1–8 (1998)
5. Catal, C.: Software fault prediction: A literature review and current trends. Expert Syst. Appl. **38**(4), 4626–4636 (2011)
6. Catal, C., Diri, B.: A fault prediction model with limited fault data to improve test process. In: Proceedings of the Product-Focused Software Process Improvement, vol. 5089, pp. 244–257 (2008)
7. Grottke, M., Trivedi, K.S.: A classification of software faults. J. Reliab. Eng. Assoc. Jpn. **27**(7), 425–438 (2005)
8. Hall, T., Beecham, S., Bowes, D., Gray, D., Counsell, S.: A systematic literature review on fault prediction performance in software engineering. IEEE Trans. Softw. Eng. **38**(6), 1276–1304 (2012)
9. Huizinga, D., Kolawa, A.: Automated Defect Prevention: Best Practices in Software Management. Wiley (2007)
10. Hryszko, J., Madeyski, L.: Cost Effectiveness of software defect prediction in an industrial project. Found. Comput. Decis. Sci. **43**(1), 7–35 (2018)
11. Jiang, Y., Cukic, B., Ma, Y.: Techniques for evaluating fault prediction models. Empir. Softw. Eng. **13**(5), 561–595 (2008)
12. Kim, S., Zhang, H., Wu, R., and Gong, L.: Dealing with noise in defect prediction. In: Proceedings of the 33rd International Conference on Software Engineering, pp. 481–490 (2011)
13. Li, N., Li, Z., Sun, X.: Classification of software defect detected by black-box testing: an empirical study. In: Proceedings of IEEE Second World Congress on Software Engineering (WCSE), vol. 2, pp. 234–240 (2010)
14. Li, P. L., Herbsleb, J., Shaw, M., Robinson, B.: Experiences and results from initiating field defect prediction and product test prioritization efforts at ABB Inc. In: Proceedings of the 28th International Conference on Software Engineering, pp. 413–422 (2006)
15. Menzies, T., DiStefano, J., Orrego, A., Chapman, R.: Assessing predictors of software defects. In: Proceedings of the Workshop Predictive Software Models, pp. 1–5 (2004)
16. Menzies, T., Milton, Z., Turhan, B., Cukic, B., Jiang, Y., Bener, A.: Defect prediction from static code features: current results, limitations, new approaches. Autom. Softw. Eng. J. **17**(4), 375–407 (2010)
17. Monden, A., Hayashi, T., Shinoda, S., Shirai, K., Yoshida, J., Barker, M., et al.: Assessing the cost effectiveness of fault prediction in acceptance testing. IEEE Trans. Softw. Eng. **39**(10), 1345–1357 (2013)
18. PROMISE: The PROMISE repository of empirical software engineering data. http://openscience.us/repo (2015)
19. Spiros Mancoridis: A Taxonomy of Bugs. Drexel University. https://www.cs.drexel.edu/~jhk39/teaching/cs576su06/L8.pdf (2010)
20. Vipindeep, V., Jalote, P.: List of Common Bugs and Programming Practices to Avoid Them. March Electronics
21. Zhou, Y., Leung, H.: Empirical analysis of object-oriented design metrics for predicting high and low severity faults. IEEE Trans. Softw. Eng. **32**(10), 771–789 (2006)

Chapter 2
Techniques Used for the Prediction of Number of Faults

Prediction of number of faults refers to the process of estimating/predicting a potential number of faults that can occur in each given software module [41]. A software module can be a class for object-oriented software, file for traditional software or any other independent component having a bunch of code bundles together. This type of prediction can be very helpful for testers to focus on the software modules having more faults. One of the most popular methods for building this type of fault prediction models is the regression. Researchers for the software fault prediction have explored a large number of regression techniques and their variations. This includes techniques such as linear regression, ridge regression, generalized linear regression, Poisson regression, negative binomial regression, etc. [46]. Study of these regression techniques showed that some techniques produced improved fault prediction performance and some techniques produced a poor performance for the same.

Identification of accurate regression techniques is the utmost requirement for building accurate and effective fault prediction model. A large number of studies have successfully applied regression techniques for the prediction of number of faults. However, there is still a dilemma about the performance of these techniques for building fault prediction model [20]. One of the reasons for this dilemma is that researchers have performed their studies on different software project datasets having different software metrics. Moreover, researchers have used different performance evaluation measures to assess the performance of these techniques. This made the comparison of regression more complicated. Therefore, it is needed to evaluate the performance of regression techniques for the common software fault datasets and using common performance evaluation measures to reach the consensus about the usefulness of these techniques.

© The Author(s), under exclusive license to Springer Nature Singapore Pte Ltd. 2019   11
S. S. Rathore and S. Kumar, *Fault Prediction Modeling for the Prediction of Number of Software Faults*, SpringerBriefs in Computer Science,
https://doi.org/10.1007/978-981-13-7131-8_2

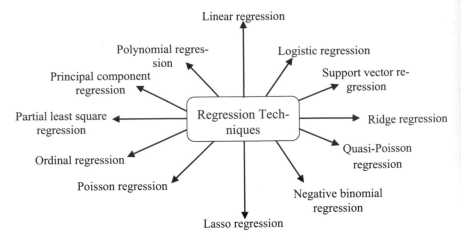

Fig. 2.1 Types of regression techniques used for the software fault prediction

2.1 Regression Techniques

Some of the regression techniques have already been explored for the fault prediction, while many of them still remain unexplored. Figure 2.1 depicts the categorization of different regression techniques. A regression technique can be univariate or can be multivariate. In univariate regression technique, there is only one independent variable and one dependent variable. In multivariate regression technique, there are more than one independent variables and one dependent variable. Most of the regression techniques are capable of handling both types of prediction scenarios.

2.1.1 Linear Regression

This type of regression technique forms a linear relationship between the independent variable(s) and the dependent variable. For the given dataset, it generates a linear equation that tries to approximate the independent variables. The performance of linear regression is prone to the presence of outliers in the dataset. It also assumes that observations in the dataset are independent and there is no multicollinearity among the independent variables [30, 52].

To estimate the regression coefficient values, it uses either least square regression or gradient descent method. The generalized equation is given as follows:

$$Y = \eta + \beta_1 x_1 + \beta_1 x_2 + \beta_3 x_3 + \cdots + \beta_n x_n \tag{2.1}$$

where β's are the weights associated with each independent variable (x) and η is the intercept value, which Y can take, if all independent variables are zero.

2.1.2 Logistic Regression

Logistic regression is used when dependent variable is of binary type (have only two categories). It fits a s-shaped curve that can take any real-values number and map it to a value between 0 and 1 [25, 29]. The generalized equation of logistic regression is given as follows:

$$Y = \frac{1}{1 + e^{-z}} \tag{2.2}$$

where z is a linear equation of independent variables.

Logistic regression is similar to the linear regression, but the curve of logistic regression is constructed using the natural logarithmic of independent variables. It overcomes the problem of normal distribution of independent variables in case of linear regression.

2.1.3 Ridge Regression

Ridge regression is used when dataset is stuffed from the multicollinearity and traditional linear regression is able to fit the curve accurately. It adds a bias to the regression estimates to reduce the standard error in the fit curve [24]. The fit regression equation by ridge regression is given as follows:

$$Y = X\beta + e \tag{2.3}$$

where Y is the dependent variable, X represents the independent variables, β is the regression coefficients to be estimated and e represents the errors are residuals.

Ridge regression uses L2 regularization to reduce the biasing. It adds L2 penalty, which is equal to the square of the magnitude of coefficients [17].

2.1.4 Polynomial Regression

It is a nonlinear type of regression, which fits a nonlinear equation by taking polynomial functions of independent variables [52]. For a single independent variable, the fit regression curve is the function of powers of single predictor by the method of least square regression. The fit curve equation of a polynomial of degree K in one variable is written as follows:

$$Y = \beta_0 + \beta_1 x + \beta_2 x^2 + \beta_3 x^3 + \cdots + \beta_n x^n + \varepsilon \tag{2.4}$$

where β's are the weights associated with features. $\{x, x^2, x^3 \ldots x^n\}$ are the new created features from the given independent variable.

In case of multiple independent variables (say x_1 and x_2), it creates new features by combining the independent variables such as the product of x_1 and x_2, i.e., $x_3 = x_1 * x_2$.

The polynomial models are generally used when the relationship between independent and dependent variables is curvilinear.

2.1.5 Principal Component Regression

Principal component regression (PCR) is used when dataset is suffered from the multicollinearity problem or when there are many independent variables in the dataset [28]. The working of PCR is two folds. In first fold, it generates principal components of the given dataset and in the next fold, it runs regression analysis on the generated principal components. Generation of principal components includes extracting new features from the dataset, which are the linear combinations of independent variables. The regression curve is fit using ordinary least square regression (linear regression) to get a vector of estimated regression coefficients. Finally, the vector of estimated regression coefficients is transformed back to the scale of actual covariates.

However, PCR fits the regression curve on the generated principal components instead of independent variables. Therefore, it is difficult to explain which independent variable is affecting the dependent variable and to what extent [34].

2.1.6 Poisson Regression

Poisson regression is the standard or base count response regression model. It is based on the Poisson probability distribution, which is the fundamental method used for modeling count response data. It assumes that the dependent variable Y has a Poisson distribution, and assumes the logarithm of its expected value can be modeled by a linear combination of independent variables. Let Y_i equal the number of faults (dependent variable) observed in a module i and X_i be a vector of independent variables for the ith observation. Given X_i, assume Y_i is Poisson distributed with the probability density function (PDF) of

$$P(Y_i | \mu_i X_i) = \frac{\mu_i^{Y_i} e^{-\mu_i}}{Y_i!} \tag{2.5}$$

where μ_i is the mean value of the dependent variable Y_i. To ensure that the expected value of μ_i is nonnegative, the link function, which displays a relationship between the expected value, and the independent variables should have the form defined by following equation [22, 31]:

$$\mu_i = e^{x_i'}\beta \tag{2.6}$$

where, β denotes the independent variables.

2.1.7 Negative Binomial Regression

Negative binomial regression is a generalized linear regression model in which the dependent variable is the count of the number of times a certain event occurs [22]. The model follows negative binomial distribution in which the mean and variance are not equal. The variance of a negative binomial distribution is defined as the function of its mean and using an additional parameter k, which is known as the dispersion parameter. Let us say that Say count of the dependent variable is Y, then the variance of Y is defined as given in equation [54]:

$$var(Y) = \mu + \mu^2/k \tag{2.7}$$

2.1.8 Partial Least Square Regression

Partial least square (PLS) regression is an alternative technique to fit the regression curve when data is highly correlated. It is also useful when there are a large number of independent variables in the dataset [1]. PLS combines the capabilities of both principal component analysis and multiple regression. PLS regression decomposes X (set of independent variables) and Y (dependent variable) as a product of a common set of orthogonal factors. The independent variables (X) are decomposed as $X = TP^l$ with $T^t T = I$. Here, T is a score matrix and P is a loading matrix. Y is decomposed as $\hat{Y} = TBC^t$. Here, B is a diagonal matrix corresponding to the regression weights and T's are the latent vectors. PLS regression finds the relations between two X and Y matrices. It tries to find the multidimensional direction in the X space that explains the maximum multidimensional variance direction in the Y space. The estimated regression curve between X and Y is given by the following equation:

$$Y = X\check{B} + \check{B}_0 \tag{2.8}$$

2.1.9   Ordinal Regression

Ordinal regression is used when dependent variable is of ordinal type, i.e., where relative ordering between different values exists. Ordinal regression is performed using a generalized linear model. It fits both a coefficient vector and a set of threshold values for the given dataset. For a set of examples in the dataset, ordinal regression finds a coefficient vector (say w) and a set of thresholds $\{\theta_1, \ldots, \theta_{K-1}\}$ such that $\{\theta_1 < \theta_2 < \ldots < \theta_{K-1}\}$. Here, a set of threshold values transforms the predicted real number values into K disjoint values, corresponding to the K labels of dependent variable [21].

The fit model is represented by the following equation:

$$P(y \leq i|x) = \sigma(\theta_i - w \cdot x) \tag{2.9}$$

where σ can be estimated by using the logistic regression function.

$$\sigma(\theta_i - w \cdot x) = \frac{1}{1 + e^{-(\theta_i - w \cdot x)}} \tag{2.10}$$

2.1.10   Quasi-Poisson Regression

Quasi-Poisson (QS) regression is a variation of negative binomial regression and it is used for the over dispersed count data. In QS regression, the variance is a linear function of mean (μ) instead of quadratic function of mean as used in negative binomial regression [54].

2.1.11   Lasso Regression

It stands for Least Absolute Shrinkage and Selection Operator regression. It is a type of linear regression and uses shrinkage scheme to fit the regression curve [33]. Where, shrinkage means that data values are shrunk towards a central point, like mean value. This regression technique is used when dataset is having high level of muticollinearity. It automatically selects certain parts of fit regression curve such as variable selection/parameter elimination. Lasso regression performs both variable selection and regularization to improve the accuracy and interpretability of the fit regression curve. It uses L1 regularization, which adds a penalty value equal to the absolute value of the magnitude of the regression coefficient. The objective function of Lasso regression is given as follows:

$$\frac{1}{N} \sum_{1}^{N} f(x_i, y_i, \alpha, \beta) \tag{2.11}$$

Lasso regression tries to minimize this objective function for α and β values. Where, α is free to take any value and β is penalized according to L1 regularization.

2.1.12 Support Vector Regression

Support vector regression (SVR) works on the principal of SVM with the provision of the real number as the predicted output. The main idea of SVR is same as SVM except in case of regression, a margin of tolerance (epsilon) is set in approximation to the SVM [7]. SVR can fit the linear as well as nonlinear regression curve for the given dataset. In the case of linear SVR, the fit curve is represented by the following equation:

$$Y = \sum_{1}^{N} (\alpha_i - \alpha_i^*) \cdot (x_i, x) + b \tag{2.12}$$

In case of nonlinear SVR, the fit curve is represented by the following equation:

$$Y = \sum_{1}^{N} (\alpha_i - \alpha_i^*) \cdot K(x_i, x) + b \tag{2.13}$$

where K is a nonlinear kernel function.

2.2 Ensemble Methods for Regression

Various researchers have evaluated the performance of regression techniques for the software fault prediction in terms of predicting the number of faults [13, 46, 50]. However, still, there is no common consent among the researchers that a particular regression technique is the most suitable for the fault prediction. Recent developments in the area of machine learning have brought the concept of ensemble learning to improve the performance of the prediction model. The goal of ensemble learning is to combine the decision of several learning models to improve the overall prediction performance of the fault prediction model [11].

In their work, Mendes-Moreira et al. [36] provided the definition of ensemble learning as "*Ensemble learning is a process that uses a set of models, each of them obtained by applying a learning process to a given problem. This set of models (ensemble) is integrated in some way to obtain the final prediction*". Ensemble methods can be used for the classification as well as the regression task. In regression, the output of the ensemble method is a number showing the potential number of faults in each software module. The ensemble learning process consists of three steps: *ensemble generation, ensemble pruning, and ensemble integration* [36]. Ensemble generation step involves the generation of a set of models for the given dataset. A number of redundant intermediate models (base learners) are generated during this step. Ensemble pruning step involves the elimination (pruning) of some model generated is the previous step. Generally, the models, which are not accurate enough or not diverse enough are pruned in this step. Finally, the ensemble integration step involves combining the generated models selected from the second step to produce the final output.

Figure 2.2 shows the classification of ensemble methods can be used for the prediction of a number of faults. Depending upon the ensemble generation process, an ensemble method can be homogeneous or heterogeneous. In the homogeneous ensemble method, a single learning technique is used to generate a set of models. Strategies such as data manipulation (subsampling of training set, manipulation of input feature, manipulating output variable, etc.), modeling process manipulation (manipulating parameters set, manipulating induction algorithm, etc.) are used to generate a set of models using same learning technique [36]. In the heterogeneous ensemble method, more than one learning techniques are used to generate a set of models. Each learning technique is trained on training dataset or part of the training dataset to generate a model. The benefit of heterogeneous ensemble methods over homogeneous ensemble methods is that earlier ones achieve more diversity in the generated set of models, which can result in improved prediction performance.

2.2.1 Homogeneous Ensemble Methods

Homogeneous ensemble methods consist of base learning models generated by a single type of the learning algorithm. In this case, ensemble based learning models can be different by the structure. A description of homogeneous ensemble methods is given as follows.

Bagging: Bagging is also known as Bootstrap Aggregating and it is proposed by Breiman [8]. The working of bagging ensemble method involves the use of subsampling of training set data manipulation scheme. In bagging ensemble, first bootstrapped subsets of training dataset are generated by selecting training examples with the replacement policy. Then, a single learning technique is trained for all the subsets of training dataset resulted in a set of models. The final prediction is performed by combining the decision of all generated models.

Boosting: Boosting ensemble method is proposed by Freund [14]. It uses an incremental learning process, where, a set of models is generated incrementally by using different example weights every time for the learning technique. Initially, the learning technique is trained for the given training dataset and misclassification information is recorded. In the subsequent step, this misclassification information is

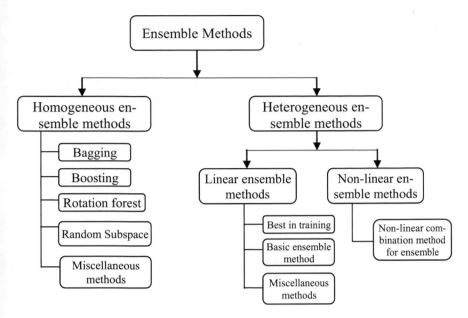

Fig. 2.2 Classification of ensemble methods

used to increase the weights of incorrectly predicted examples. The weights update is carried out in such a way that error of incorrectly predicted examples is counted heavily in the next iterations. This process of model building is repeated for M iterations. The final prediction is done by combining the output of each generated model.

Random subspace: Random subspace ensemble method uses manipulation of input feature data manipulation scheme for the generation of a set of models. It creates a set of models by partitioning the input features into different subsets. Learning technique (usually tree-based technique) is training for each subset to generate one model. The partition of input features is carried out uniformly and randomly to reduce bias. The final prediction is performed by combining the decision of generated decision trees [23]. Working of the random subspace method is inspired by the working of bagging. However, it uses the manipulation of input feature instead of manipulation of the training set.

Rotation forest: Rotation forest ensemble method use the concept of PCA (principal component analysis) to select features and examples of the training set before building the decision trees [35, 48]. Initially, the feature set of training dataset is partitioned into K disjoint subsets of approximately equal size. Then, it randomly removes 25% of examples from the training set using a bootstrap method. PCA is used for the rest of 75% of training examples. This process is repeated M times and each time a separate tree is generated. The final prediction is made by combining the outputs of each tree.

Stacking: Stacking ensemble method is based on the concept of meta-learner. It uses a two steps process for ensemble model building. In the first step, it generates a set of models by training learning technique for the training dataset. This step is called level-0. In the second step, it combines generate models by using another learning technique known as the meta-model. This step is called level-1. The output of the meta-model is the final output of the ensemble method [57].

2.2.2 Heterogeneous Ensemble Methods

In heterogeneous ensemble methods, more than one learning techniques are used to generate a set of models. Depending upon the way decisions of these learning techniques are combined, heterogeneous ensemble methods are classified into two types: linear ensemble methods and nonlinear ensemble methods [47].

In linear ensemble methods, ensemble integration is performed using a linear combination of the learning technique predictions. The generalized equation of linear ensemble method is given as follows:

$$\hat{f}_{\text{int}} \sum_{i=1}^{N} w_i(x) * p_i(x) \tag{2.14}$$

where, $\hat{f}_{\text{int}}$ is an integration function and N are the number of learning techniques used. $w_i(x)$'s are the weights associated with each model and $p_i(x)$'s are the prediction made by learning techniques.

A brief description of linear ensemble methods is given as follows.

Basic ensemble method: This ensemble method calculates mean of the prediction of all generated ensemble models. The ensemble output is given as follows [44]:

$$\hat{f}_{\text{int}} = \frac{1}{N} \sum_{i=1}^{N} p_i(x) \tag{2.15}$$

This method assumes that errors of the models are mutually independent and have mean zero.

Best in training (BIT): BIT ensemble method is based on the assumption that each learning technique performs differently for different partitions of training dataset [32]. Among the generated ensemble models using learning techniques, BIT ensemble method selects the model that has performed the best in the training dataset using some performance measures. The output of the selected model is then use as the output of ensemble method.

Error rate weighted average ensemble method (ERWT): ERWT ensemble method uses relative error rate value to calculate the weights of generated ensemble models [37]. All the generated ensemble models are applied to the validation dataset and their performance is recorded in terms of relative error rate value. Next, the cumulative correctness of each ensemble model is calculated. The correctness value of each learning technique is defined as the negative of relative error rate value. The cumulative correctness values are used to calculate the weights of generated ensemble models, which show the contribution of ensemble models. Finally, weight values are used to combine the prediction outputs of ensemble models for the final prediction. Final output of ERWT is stated by the following equation:

$$\text{Ensemble output} = \sum_{i=1}^{N} CC_i * p_i(x) \tag{2.16}$$

where CC is the cumulative correctness of generated ensemble models and $P(x)$ is the predicted value of faults of ensemble models for testing dataset.

Linear regression based ensemble method (LRWT): In LRWT ensemble method, linear regression is used to combine the outputs of the ensemble models [32]. Initially, all the generated ensemble models are applied to the validation dataset and predicted an estimated value of faults for the given examples in the validation dataset. This predicted value of the number of faults by each ensemble model is considered as independent variables and actual value of faults in validation dataset is considered as the dependent variable. Next, linear regression is used to model the relationship between the independent and dependent variables in the form of a function $F(x)$. Last, the parameters estimated by linear regression show the weights of the learning techniques to be used for final prediction. The final output of LRWT is stated by the following equation:

$$\text{Ensemble output} = \sum_{i=1}^{N} w_i * N_f^i + w_0 \tag{2.17}$$

where w_i's are the weights of generated ensemble models and N_f^i is the predicted value of faults is ensemble models for testing dataset. w_0 is the intercept value.

Nonlinear ensemble method: In nonlinear ensemble method, a nonlinear technique is used to establish the relationship between input values and output values. Initially, all the generated ensemble models are applied to the validation datasets and their predicted numbers of fault values are recorded. The used nonlinear technique takes the outputs of the ensemble models for the validation dataset as the input for the training and uses the outputs of the ensemble models for test dataset as the dependent variable to perform the final prediction. The final output of the ensemble method will be the output of the nonlinear technique for testing dataset. Techniques such as regression forest and gradient boosting regression can be used for nonlinear ensemble methods [47].

2.3   State-of-Art of Regression and Ensemble Methods for the Prediction of Number of Faults

There is a great amount of work available related to the prediction of a number of faults in given software systems using regression techniques [18, 41, 19]. This includes the use of techniques such as linear regression and its variants, Poisson regression [15], negative binomial regression [22], genetic programming [2], support vector regression [7], etc. Recently, the use of ensemble methods (homogeneous as well as heterogeneous) also gained popularity for the software fault prediction [12, 39, 60]. Most of these studies include the evaluation of bagging, boosting, and random forest ensemble methods, whereas other ensemble methods are rarely explored. This section discusses the present scenario of regression techniques and ensemble methods for the prediction of number of faults.

Grave et al. [18] presented an initial work for the prediction of number of faults. Authors built fault prediction models using generalized linear regression (GLR) and applied them over a large telecommunications system for the evaluation. Authors extracted various change and history-related software metrics from the used software system and built models. Experiment results favored the use of module age, changes made to a module, and age of the change software metrics for the best fault prediction accuracy. Additionally, it has been found that other used software metrics such as the size of a module and complexity are not accurate enough for the fault-proneness prediction in the given software system. However, authors did not provide any comprehensive evaluation of GLR technique for the prediction of a number of faults.

In another attempt to build the prediction models for the prediction of number of faults in the software system, Ostrand et al. presented some studies using negative binomial regression (NBR) technique [40–42]. In Ostrand et al. [41], authors built and evaluated the fault prediction model using different software file characteristics and LOC metrics extracted from two industrial software systems. Results of the experimental analysis showed that NBR-based fault prediction model produced an accurate performance for a number of faults prediction. However, the presented prediction model was complex and difficult to build. To handle this issue, authors presented a simplified LOC metric based fault prediction model. The simplified model demonstrated a comparable fault prediction performance as achieved by the full model, while a significant reduction in the model building effort has been reported for the simplified model. The presented study has been suffered from the limited evaluation of results as authors used only one performance measure (faults found in the top 20% of the files). Other works reported by Ostrand et al. such as [40] and [8] also presented NBR based fault prediction models and discussed the results. These works also showed that presented models produced a significant performance for the software fault prediction.

Some other works have also evaluated the use of NBR technique for the software fault prediction such as [26, 59]. In Janes et al. [26], a NBR-based fault prediction model has been presented that uses several object-oriented metrics extracted from a large telecommunication system. Experimental results showed that the NBR based fault prediction model was able to produce significant accuracy for the number of faults prediction. In Yu [59], authors presented two different fault prediction models, one is NBR-based model and another one is logistic regression based model and compared their performance for the software fault prediction. NBR-based fault prediction model showed better results when predicting multiple faults in a software module, whereas, logistic regression based fault prediction model performed better when predicting fault-prone software modules.

Fagundes et al. [13] presented a zero-inflated Poisson regression based fault prediction model for the prediction of number of faults in the software system. Authors performed an experimental study for eight NASA fault datasets and evaluated results using the mean magnitude of relative error performance measure. Authors compared the performance of presented prediction mode with several machine learning techniques and found that presented fault prediction model performed significantly better in comparison to other used techniques.

Gao and Khoshgoftaaar [15] performed a comparative evaluation of five different count models, namely, Poisson regression, negative binomial regression, zero-inflated negative binomial regression, zero-inflated Poisson regression, and hurdle negative binomial regression for the prediction of number of faults. Each count model-based fault prediction model is built for two industrial software systems using different complexity and object-oriented software metrics. Experimental evidence showed that zero-inflated negative binomial regression and hurdle negative binomial regression models outperformed other used count models for the prediction of number of faults. In another study, Khoshgoftaar and Gao [51] developed two count models (Poisson regression and zero-inflated Poisson) based fault prediction models and one logistic regression based fault prediction model for qualitative and quantitative prediction of faults in software systems. An experimental analysis for a large military telecommunication system (CCCS) having various product metrics has been reported. Results found that Poisson and zero-inflated Poisson-based fault prediction models produced similar classification accuracies as the logistic regression based prediction model. For the prediction of number of faults, the zero-inflated model produced better prediction accuracy than the Poisson model.

In an attempt to explore the use of the search-based technique for the software fault prediction, Afzal et al. [2] presented a fault prediction model using genetic programming technique. Authors reported case studies for three different industrial software systems and built fault prediction models using reported weekly fault counts in software system as independent variable. Experimental results favored the use of genetic programming for fault count prediction in software systems. Rathore and Kumar [45] also reported an empirical study evaluating the effectiveness of genetic programming for the number of software faults prediction. Authors also concluded that genetic programming produced significant fault prediction results with lower misclassification errors and thus could be a good candidate for building fault prediction model. Pai and Dugan [43] performed an empirical analysis for software fault content and fault-proneness prediction using Bayesian methods. Additionally, authors showed how multiple linear regression, Poisson regression, and logistic regression could be modeled as Bayesian network (BN). Results from the BN model showed that the model estimated as BN performed accurately and did not differ significantly from the ground data at a statistically significant level. Later, Afzal et al. [58] presented a fault prediction model that uses an adaptive ranking approach to rank source files with respect to the likelihood of bug occurrence. The presented model uses the "knowledge of functional decomposition of source code, API descriptions of library components, bug fixing history, code change history, and file dependency graph" software metrics. Results of the experimental study for six large open source projects showed that presented ranking approach yielded better performance compared to other state-of-the-art techniques used for software fault prediction.

Recently, some researchers built software fault prediction models using ensemble methods. These studies mainly include ensemble methods such as bagging, boosting, voting, random forest, etc. [3, 4, 12]. Few studies also explored heterogeneous ensemble methods for software fault prediction [38, 46, 53]. Misirli et al. [33] reported an ensemble method for the software fault prediction that involved the use of naive Bayes, artificial neural network and voting feature intervals as the base learners. Additionally, the authors analyzed the use of different combination rules to combine base learner outputs for the ensemble. Presented ensemble methods produced improved prediction accuracy and outperformed other used individual techniques. Zheng [60] presented three cost-sensitive boosting algorithms using the neural network as the base learner for software defect prediction. The performance of presented ensemble methods has been evaluating via an experimental study for four NASA datasets and results showed that the presented ensemble method achieved improved prediction performance for software defect prediction.

In another study, Twala [53] built and evaluated ensemble methods for software fault prediction using different machine learning techniques as base learners. The study was performed for a large space software system, results found that presented ensemble methods with the decision tree, and apriori techniques as base learners yielded better performance than other used fault prediction techniques. Overall, decision tree and naive Bayes techniques performed relatively better than other machine learning techniques. Wang et al. [56] performed a comparative study of some ensemble methods for the software fault prediction. The study includes bagging, boosting, random forest, voting, and stacking ensemble methods. Results revealed that overall ensemble methods performed better as compared to individual fault prediction techniques, and out of used ensemble methods voting and random forest produced the best prediction performance. In another study, Alijamann et al. [3] built fault prediction models using bagging and boosting ensemble methods and compared the performance of these methods with some individual fault prediction techniques. Experimental results showed the superiority of ensemble methods over the used individual fault prediction techniques and recommended to use ensemble methods for software fault prediction.

Recently Elish et al. [12], explored the use of ensemble methods for software maintenance and change prediction. Authors build three different homogeneous and heterogeneous ensemble methods using four different base learning techniques for the ensemble. They investigated different combination rules for the ensemble method. The performance of presented ensemble methods has been evaluated via an experimental analysis for two public datasets, and results found that best-in-training based heterogeneous ensemble method outperformed other used ensemble methods. Overall, presented ensemble methods produced better or at least comparable performance as compared to individual learning techniques. Siers and Islam [49] presented a decision tree-based cost-sensitive ensemble method named CSForest and a cost-sensitive voting technique named CSVoting for the software defect prediction. To assess the capability of presented ensemble methods, authors performed an experimental analysis for six publicly available fault datasets and compared the performance of presented methods with six classification algorithms. Results of the analysis showed the proficiency of presented methods compared to the used classification techniques and recommended to use these techniques to reduce the misclassification cost in software fault prediction. Mausa et al. [35] presented a rotation forest ensemble method, which uses PCA (program component analysis) to select a subset of the dataset for each iteration of model building. Authors built and evaluated prediction models for five subsequent releases of Eclipse JDT project and compared the performance of the presented ensemble method with logistic regression and random forest. Results showed that presented rotation forest ensemble methods performed significantly accurate for the software fault prediction. Bal and Kumar [5] explored the use of extreme learning machine (ELM) to predict the number of faults in the software systems. Authors have proposed linear homogeneous ensemble models for two variations of ELM, Differentiable Extreme Learning Machine Ensemble (DELME) and Non-differentiable Extreme Learning Machine Ensemble (NELME) to predict the number of software faults. Further, the authors investigated the use of ELM and nonlinear heterogeneous ensemble using ELM for software defect prediction. The presented ensemble methods were evaluated by performing an experimental case study for several software fault datasets collected from the PROMISE and eclipse data repositories. Additionally, authors explored the use of extreme learning machine (ELM) and ELM based nonlinear heterogeneous ensemble methods for cross-project software fault prediction [6]. Authors found that the presented ELM based nonlinear heterogeneous ensemble model provided better prediction accuracy as compared to the single fault prediction models.

2.4 Performance Evaluation Measures

Once software fault prediction model is built, the next task is to assess its performance for some unseen examples (testing dataset) for unbiased evaluation. Here, fault prediction modeling follows a supervised model building process, where the dependent variable (number of faults) information is already available. We can use this ground truth information to compare the predicted values of faults with the actual value of faults and assess the performance of the prediction model. Performance evaluation measures are used for this task. Initially, original fault dataset is partitioned into the training dataset and testing dataset and then a fault prediction model is trained for the training dataset. Various performance evaluation measures are available that can be used to assess the performance of fault prediction model. In our fault prediction model, the dependent variable is of continuous type (regression), therefore, we have used error based performance evaluation measures. The used performance measures compared the predicted values of number of faults with the corresponding actual values of number of faults [27]. Details of performance evaluation measures are given in this subsection [10, 46].

(i) *Mean Absolute Error (MAE)*: This measure first calculates the corresponding difference between the predicted values of faults and the actual values of faults and then show the summarized mean value for all testing examples. It shows the uncertainty in the prediction performance of the model. Equation 2.18 defines it.

$$\text{MAE} = \frac{1}{T} \sum_{i=1}^{T} |\overline{Y}_i - Y_i| \tag{2.18}$$

where $\overline{Y}_i$ shows the predicted value of number of faults for a software module and Y_i shows the corresponding actual value of number of faults. T is the total number of modules in the software system.

(ii) *Mean relative error (MRE)*: This measure first calculates the corresponding difference between the predicted values of faults and the actual values of faults and then calculate how large error is in comparison to the actual value of faults. It summarizes the mean value of this measure for all testing examples. Equation 2.19 defines it.

$$\text{MRE} = \frac{1}{T} \sum_{i=1}^{T} \frac{|\overline{Y}_i - Y_i|}{(Y_i + 1)} \tag{2.19}$$

A value "1" is added with the Y_i value in the denominator to avoid the effect of zero values that can appear in the actual value of faults part. This makes the calculation of MRE always well-defined [51].

(iii) *Prediction at level l or Pred(l)*: This performance measure determines, how accurately a prediction model detects faults in the smaller number of software modules. It calculates the fraction of predicted values having MRE values under a certain threshold level [55]. It counts all number of examples (software modules) whose MRE values are within *l*% threshold of the actual value. Generally, it is recommended to keep the value of *l* less than 30% [46]. Equation 2.20 defines it.

$$\text{Pred}(l) = K/T \tag{2.20}$$

where K is the total number of modules whose values are less than or equal to *l*. *T* is the total number of software modules. *l* is the threshold value. In this presented experimental analysis, we have used 0.30 as the value of *l*.

2.5 Summary

Predicting the potential number of faults in software modules can help in ranking these modules according to their prediction content and help in the optimized allocation of testing resources. Additionally, it can help in the defection and fixing of more faults when given the limited testing resources. In this chapter, we discussed various techniques used earlier for the prediction of number of faults. Further, we described different ensemble methods for the regression. State-of-the-art about the techniques used for the prediction of number of faults is also presented in the chapter. At the end of the chapter, we presented performance measures used for the evaluation of built fault prediction models.

References

1. Abdi, H.: Partial least square regression (PLS regression). Encycl. Res. Methods Soc. Sci. **6**(4), 792–795 (2003)
2. Afzal, W., Torkar, R., Feldt, R.: Prediction of fault count data using genetic programming. In: Proceedings of IEEE International Multitopic Conference, INMIC, pp. 349–356 (2008)
3. Aljamaan, H., Elish, M.O., et al.: An empirical study of bagging and boosting ensembles for identifying faulty classes in object-oriented software. In: CIDM 2009, IEEE Symposium on Computational Intelligence and Data Mining, pp. 187–194 (2009)
4. Arar, O.F., Ayan, K.: Software defect prediction using cost-sensitive neural network. Appl. Soft Comput. **33**, 263–277 (2015)
5. Bal, P., Kumar, S.: Extreme learning machine based linear homogeneous ensemble for software fault prediction. In Proceedings of 13th International Conference on Software Technologies (ICSOFT 2018), pp. 69–78 (2018a)
6. Bal, P., Kumar, S.: Cross project software defect prediction using extreme learning machine: an ensemble based study. In: Proceedings of 13th International Conference on Software Technologies (ICSOFT 2018), pp. 320–327 (2018b)
7. Basak, D., Pal, S., Patranabis, D.C.: Support vector regression. Neural Inf. Process. Lett. Rev. **11**(10), 203–224 (2007)
8. Bell, R.M., Ostrand, T.J., Weyuker, E.J.: Looking for bugs in all the right places. In Proceedings of the 2006 International Symposium on Software testing and Analysis, ACM, pp. 61–72 (2006)
9. Breiman, L.: Bagging predictors. Mach. Learn. **24**(2), 123–140 (1996)
10. Conte, S.D., Dunsmore, H.E., Shen, V.Y.: Software Engineering Metrics and Models. Benjamin-Cummings Publishing Co., Inc (1986)
11. Dietterich, T.G.: Ensemble methods in machine learning. In: International Workshop on Multiple Classifier Systems. Springer, Berlin, Heidelberg, pp. 1–15 (2000)
12. Elish, M.O., Aljamaan, H., Ahmad, I.: Three empirical studies on predicting software maintainability using ensemble methods. Soft Comput. **19**(9), 1–14 (2015)
13. Fagundes, R.A., Souza, R.M., Cysneiros, F.J.: Zero-inflated prediction model in software-fault data. IET Softw. **10**(1), 1–9 (2016)
14. Freund, Y.: Boosting a weak learning algorithm by majority. In: Proceedings of COLT, vol. 90, pp. 202–216 (1990)
15. Gao, K., Khoshgoftaar, T.M.: A comprehensive empirical study of count models for software fault prediction. IEEE Trans. Reliab. **56**(2), 223–236 (2007)
16. Gardner, W., Mulvey, E.P., Shaw, E.C.: Regression analyses of counts and rates: Poisson, overdispersed Poisson, and negative binomial models. Psychol. Bull. **118**(3), 392 (1995)

17. Girard, D.A.: Asymptotic optimality of the fast randomized versions of GCV and C_L in ridge regression and regularization. Ann. Stat. **19**(4), 1950–1963 (1991)
18. Graves, T.L., Karr, A.F., Marron, J.S., Siy, H.: Predicting fault incidence using software change history. IEEE Trans. Softw. Eng. **26**(7), 653–661 (2000)
19. Gyimothy, T., Ferenc, R., Siket, I.: Empirical validation of object-oriented metrics on open source software for fault prediction. IEEE Trans. Softw. Eng. **31**(10), 897–910 (2005)
20. Hall, T., Beecham, S., Bowes, D., Gray, D., Counsell, S.: A systematic literature review on fault prediction performance in software engineering. IEEE Trans. Softw. Eng. **38**(6), 1276–1304 (2012)
21. Hedeker, D., Gibbons, R.D.: A random-effects ordinal regression model for multilevel analysis. Biometrics, 933–944 (1994)
22. Hilbe, J.M.: Negative Binomial Regression, 2nd edn. Jet Propulsion Laboratory, California Institute of Technology and Arizona State University (2012)
23. Ho, T.K.: The random subspace method for constructing decision forests. IEEE Trans. Pattern Anal. Mach. Intell. **20**(8), 832–844 (1998)
24. Hoerl, A.E., Kennard, R.W.: Ridge regression: biased estimation for nonorthogonal problems. Technometrics **12**(1), 55–67 (1970)
25. Hosmer Jr, D.W., Lemeshow, S., & Sturdivant, R.X.: Applied logistic regression, vol. 398. Wiley (2013)
26. Janes, A., Scotoo, M., Pedrycz, W., Russo, B., Stefanovic, M., Succi, G.: Identification of defect-prone classes in telecommunication software systems using design metrics. Inf. Sci. **176**(24), 3711–3734 (2006)
27. Jiang, Y., Cukic, B., Ma, Y.: Techniques for evaluating fault prediction models. Empir. Softw. Eng. **13**(5), 561–595 (2008)
28. Jolliffe, I.T.: A note on the use of principal components in regression. Appl. Stat. **31**(3), 300–303 (1982)
29. Kleinbaum, D.G., Klein, M.: Logistic Regression: A Self-learning Text. Springer Science & Business Media (2010)
30. Kutner, M.H., Nachtsheim, C., Neter, J.: Applied Linear Regression Models. McGraw-Hill/Irwin (2004)
31. Lambert, D.: Zero-inflated Poisson regression, with an application to defects in manufacturing. Technometrics **34**(1), 1–14 (1992)
32. LeBlanc, M., Tibshirani, R.: Combining estimates in regression and classification. J. Am. Stat. Assoc. **91**(436), 1641–1650 (1996)
33. Li, W., Feng, J., Jiang, T.: IsoLasso: a LASSO regression approach to RNA-Seq based transcriptome assembly. In: International Conference on Research in Computational Molecular Biology. Springer, Berlin, Heidelberg, pp. 168–188 (2011)
34. Liu, R.X., Kuang, J., Gong, Q., Hou, X.L.: Principal component regression analysis with SPSS. Comput. Methods Programs Biomed. **71**(2), 141–147 (2003)
35. Mauša, G., Bogunović, N., Grbac, T.G., Bašić, B.D.: Rotation forest in software defect prediction. In: Proceedings of 4th Workshop on Software Quality Analysis, Monitoring, Improvement, and Applications SQAMIA, pp. 35 (2015)
36. Mendes-Moreira, J., Soares, C., Jorge, A.M., Sousa, J.F.D.: Ensemble approaches for regression: A survey. ACM Comput. Surv. (CSUR) **45**(1), 10 (2012)
37. Merz, C.J.: Classification and regression by combining models. PhD thesis, University of California Irvine (1998)
38. Mısırlı, A.T., Bener, A.B., Turhan, B.: An industrial case study of classifier ensembles for locating software defects. Softw. Qual. J. **19**(3), 515–536 (2011)
39. Mousavi, R., Eftekhari, M.: A new ensemble learning methodology based on hybridization of classifier ensemble selection approaches. Appl. Soft Comput. **37**, 652–666 (2015)
40. Ostrand, T.J., Weyuker, E.J., Bell, R.M.: Where the bugs are. ACM SIGSOFT Softw. Eng. Notes **29**(4), 86–96 (2004)
41. Ostrand, T.J., Weyuker, E.J., Bell, R.M.: Predicting the location and number of faults in large software systems. IEEE Trans. Softw. Eng. **31**(4), 340–355 (2005)

42. Ostrand, T.J., Weyuker, E.J., Bell, R.M.: Looking for bugs in all the right places. In: Proceedings of the International Symposium on Software Testing and Analysis, pp. 61–72 (2006)
43. Pai, G.J., Dugan, J.B.: Empirical analysis of software fault content and fault proneness using Bayesian methods. IEEE Trans. Softw. Eng. **33**(10), 675–686 (2007)
44. Perrone, M.P., Cooper, L.N.: When networks disagree: ensemble methods for hybrid neural networks (No. TR-61). Brown Univ Providence RI Inst for Brain and Neural Systems (1992)
45. Rathore, S.S., Kumar, S.: Predicting number of faults in software system using genetic programming. Procedia Comput. Sci. **62**, 303–311 (2015)
46. Rathore S.S., & Kumar, S.: An empirical study of some software fault prediction techniques for the number of faults prediction. Soft Comput. **21**(24), 7417–7434 (2017a)
47. Rathore, S.S., Kumar, S.: Linear and non-linear heterogeneous ensemble methods to predict the number of faults in software systems. Knowl. Based Syst. **119**, 232–256 (2017b)
48. Rodriguez, J.J., Kuncheva, L.I., Alonso, C.J.: Rotation forest: a new classifier ensemble method. IEEE Trans. Pattern Anal. Mach. Intell. **28**(10), 1619–1630 (2006)
49. Siers, M.J., Islam, M.Z.: Software defect prediction using a cost sensitive decision forest and voting, and a potential solution to the class imbalance problem. Inf. Syst. **51**, 62–71 (2015)
50. Khoshgoftaar, T.M., Geleyn, E., Nguyen, L.: Empirical case studies of combining software quality classification models. In Proceedings of 3rd International Conference on Quality Software, pp. 40–49 (2003)
51. Khoshgoftaar, T.M., Gao, K.: Count models for software quality estimation. IEEE Trans. Reliab. **56**(2), 212–222 (2007)
52. Theil, H.: A rank-invariant method of linear and polynomial regression analysis. Henri Theil's Contributions to Economics and Econometrics, pp. 345–381. Springer, Dordrecht (1992)
53. Twala, B.: Predicting software faults in large space systems using machine learning techniques. Def. Sci. J. **61**(4), 306–316 (2011)
54. Ver Hoef, J.M., Boveng, P.L.: Quasi-Poisson vs. negative binomial regression: how should we model overdispersed count data? Ecology **88**(11), 2766–2772 (2007)
55. Veryard, R.: The Economics of Information Systems and Software. Butterworth-Heinemann (2014)
56. Wang, T., Li, W., Shi, H., Liu, Z.: Software defect prediction based on classifiers ensemble. J. Inf. Comput. Sci. **8**(16), 4241–4254 (2011)
57. Wolpert, D.H.: Stacked generalization. Neural networks **5**(2), 241–259 (1992)
58. Ye, X., Bunescu, R., Liu, C.: Mapping bug reports to relevant files: a ranking model, a fine-grained benchmark, and feature evaluation. IEEE Trans. Softw. Eng. **42**(4), 379–402 (2016)
59. Yu, L.: Using negative binomial regression analysis to predict software faults: a study of apache ant. Int. J. Inf. Technol. Comput. Sci. **4**(8), 63–70 (2012)
60. Zheng, J.: Cost-sensitive boosting neural networks for software defect prediction. Expert. Syst. Appl. **37**(6), 4537–4543 (2010)

Chapter 3
Homogeneous Ensemble Methods for the Prediction of Number of Faults

Software testing is intended to find bugs/faults that can occur in the software components currently under development. Software fault prediction (SFP) helps in achieving this goal by predicting the probability of fault occurrence in the software modules
before the testing phase. This automated nature of SFP can help testers/developers to
find faults effectively and help product managers to make effective decisions about
the allotment of limited software development resources efficiently [1]. Software
fault dataset augmented with various software metrics and fault information is generally used to build the fault prediction models. Depending upon the aim of the
prediction, a model can label software modules into faulty and non-faulty classes or
predict a potential number of faults that can occur in a software module [8].

A large number of studies have already been published focusing on predicting
faulty and non-faulty labels of software modules. However, this type of prediction
provides only limited information about the fault-proneness of software modules [3].
Prediction of the number of faults in each software module provides more comprehensive information about the fault-proneness of software modules, which can be
used to make optimal use of software development resources [10]. A considerable
number of studies have been reported in the literature for the prediction of number of
faults in the software modules. However, the dispersed nature of these studies made
it difficult to draw any generalized conclusions from them. Moreover, these studies
showed that there is no silver bullet technique or approach that can be used across
different software systems to predict number of faults effectively and efficiently.
Recent research on software fault prediction advocated the use of ensemble methods
to build effective and accurate prediction models [13]. Therefore, we explore the use
of ensemble methods for software fault prediction and report the findings.

© The Author(s), under exclusive license to Springer Nature Singapore Pte Ltd. 2019   31
S. S. Rathore and S. Kumar, *Fault Prediction Modeling for the Prediction
of Number of Software Faults*, SpringerBriefs in Computer Science,
https://doi.org/10.1007/978-981-13-7131-8_3

3.1 Homogeneous Ensemble Methods

Conceptually, the ensemble method is a combination of more than one learning techniques (known as base learners) with the aim to improve the overall prediction accuracy or performance. It utilizes the prediction capability of each intermediate learning technique for the given dataset and combines their capabilities to improve the overall prediction. Depending on the use of learning techniques in building ensemble method, an ensemble method can be homogeneous or heterogeneous [9]. In homogeneous ensemble methods, a single learning technique is used. Multiple variants of the single learning technique (each of them serves as an intermediate prediction model) are generated by manipulating the dataset features or examples. Final prediction is performed by combining the prediction of all generated variants of a single learning technique [4, 9].

The previous chapter discusses different homogeneous ensemble methods in details. In this study, we have used five different homogeneous ensemble methods, bagging, boosting, random subspace, rotation forest, and stacking to build the software fault prediction models. For each ensemble method, we have used three different learning techniques as base learners. A detailed description of these learning techniques is given by Rathore and Kumar [11].

3.2 Evaluation of Homogeneous Ensemble Methods

We performed an experimental analysis and evaluated the performance of homogeneous ensemble methods for the prediction of number of faults. The elements of experimental analysis are described in the upcoming subsections.

3.2.1 Software Fault Datasets

One of the requirements to increase the reliability of results of an experimental analysis is the repeatability of the experiment results. A large number of earlier studies related to the prediction of number of faults have not been used benchmarked datasets, which made it difficult to replicate their findings. Due to this reason, in this work, we have used benchmarked software fault datasets available in the PROMISE data repository [2]. PROMISE data repository is a publically available data repository, which contains software fault datasets of various open-source software projects among other software process related datasets. Currently, it hosts software fault datasets corresponding to 65 different software projects including their different releases/versions. The size of these fault datasets varies from few hundred software modules to thousand software modules. Here, a software module represents a class for object-oriented (OO) software system. In our work, we focused on OO software systems only. All the used fault datasets contained the same 20 object-oriented software metrics. They are—"weighted method count (WMC), coupling between objects (CBO), response for a class (RFC), depth of inheritance tree (DIT), number of children (NOC), inheritance coupling (IC), coupling between methods (CBM), afferent coupling (CA), efferent coupling (CE), measure of functional abstraction (MFA), lack of cohesion of methods (LCOM), lack of cohesion of methods 3 (LCOM3), cohesion among methods (CAM), measure of aggregation (MOA), number of public methods in a class (NPM), data access metric (DAM), average method complexity (AMC), lines of code (LOC), cyclomatic complexity (CC)". Jureczko and Madeyski [7] has reported a detailed discussion of these metrics. Earlier literature related to the evaluation of software metrics for software fault prediction found that software metrics related to the object-oriented features of software systems performed significantly accurate for the fault prediction [5, 12]. Based on this argument, we included only those fault datasets in our study having OO software metrics. The experimental study includes 28 different software fault datasets out of total fault datasets available in the PROMISE data repository. We have discarded fault datasets having less than 300 software modules. The reason to exclude some fault datasets is that smaller fault datasets may not be representing comprehensive fault occurring pattern in the software system and thus it is difficult to trust results of these datasets. An overview of used software fault datasets is given in Table 3.1. We have used multiple releases/versions of each given software project to build and evaluate fault prediction models.

Each used fault dataset contained a unique module ID, class path of the software module, 20 OO metrics (independent variables), and number of faults occurred information. We preprocessed fault datasets and removed the unique ID and path to the software module fields from the datasets. We have applied the same preprocess and transformation for all the used 28 fault datasets.

3.2.2 Experimental Setup

As given in Table 3.1, the percentage of faulty software modules in the used software faults datasets vary between 3.82 and 98.68%. This variation in the fault percentage can affect the performance of ensemble methods used for the prediction model building. To analyze this effect on the performance of ensemble methods, we first categorized the fault datasets into four different groups based the percentage of the faulty modules and then evaluated the performance of all ensemble methods for each group. Details about different groups of software fault datasets are given in Table 3.2. Group-1 contains all the fault datasets having the percentage of faulty software modules below 10%. Fault datasets have faulty software modules between 10 and 20% categorized into group-2. Fault datasets have faulty software modules between 20 and 30% categorized into group-3. Group-4 contains all the fault datasets have 30% or more faulty software modules.

Table 3.1 Description of used software fault datasets (dataset can be referred from Kumar and Rathore [8])

Dataset release		Number of faults	Total number of modules	Total number of faulty modules	% Of faulty modules	# Non-commented-LOC
Ant	Ant-1.7	338	746	166	22.25%	208KLOC
Camel	Camel-1.0	14	340	13	3.82%	33KLOC
	Camel-1.2	522	609	216	35.47%	66KLOC
	Camel-1.4	335	873	145	16.61%	98KLOC
	Camel-1.6	500	966	188	19.46%	113KLOC
Ivy	Ivy-2.0	56	353	40	11.33%	87KLOC
Jedit	Jedit-4.0	226	307	75	24.43%	144KLOC
	Jedit-4.1	217	313	79	25.24%	153KLOC
	Jedit-4.2	106	368	48	13.04%	170KLOC
	Jedit-4.3	12	493	11	2.23%	202KLOC
Lucene	Lucene-2.4	632	341	203	59.53%	102KLOC
Poi	Poi-2.0	39	315	37	11.75%	93KLOC
	Poi-2.5	519	386	248	64.25%	119KLOC
	Poi-3.0	500	443	281	63.43%	129KLOC
Prop	Prop-1	5493	18472	2738	14.82%	3816KLOC
	Prop-2	4096	23015	2431	10.56%	3748KLOC
	Prop-3	1640	10275	1180	11.48%	1604KLOC
	Prop-4	1362	8719	840	9.63%	1508KLOC
	Prop-5	1930	8517	1299	15.25%	1081KLOC
	Prop-6	79	661	66	9.98%	97KLOC
Tomcat	–	114	859	77	8.96%	300KLOC
Xalan	Xalan-2.4	156	724	111	15.33%	225KLOC
	Xalan-2.5	531	804	387	48.13%	304KLOC
	Xalan-2.6	625	886	411	46.39%	411KLOC
	Xalan-2.7	1213	910	898	98.68%	428KLOC
Xerces	Xerces-1.2	115	441	71	16.10%	159KLOC
	Xerces-1.3	193	454	69	15.20%	167KLOC
	Xerces-1.4	1596	589	437	74.19%	141KLOC"

Table 3.2 Categorization of used software fault datasets based on the percentage of faulty modules

Category	Percentage of faulty software modules	Number of software fault datasets
Category-1	Less than 10%	5
Category-2	10–20%	12
Category-3	20–30%	3
Category-4	Above 30%	8

3.2.3 Experimental Procedure

The experimental procedure adopted for building and evaluating ensemble methods based fault prediction models is given in Table 3.3. We have used a 10-folds cross-validation scheme to build and evaluate prediction models.

3.2.4 Tools and Techniques Used for Experiment

We have used Weka machine learning tool to run the experiments. All the used ensemble methods are implemented in the Weka tool [6]. We have used that implementation of methods and built the fault prediction models. Additionally, we have used three different learning techniques as base learners to the ensemble methods. The implementation of these learning techniques is also available in the Weka tool.

We have used mean absolute error (MAE), mean relative error (MRE), and pred(0.30) performance measures to evaluate the performance of ensemble methods based fault prediction models. The description of these performance measures is given in Chap. 2, Sect. 2.3.

3.3 Results and Discussion

We have applied each homogeneous ensemble method using each base learning technique to all fault datasets listed in Table 3.1. Since we have used five different ensemble methods, each of which used three base learning techniques, so total 15 ensemble-based fault prediction models have been built for each fault dataset. We grouped results into four different groups as identified in Table 3.2 and reported results in terms of mean absolute error (MAE) and mean relative error (MRE). Tables 3.4, 3.5, 3.6, and 3.7 show results of the experimental analysis. Each table is corresponding to one group of software fault datasets and shows results of MAE and MRE. For each performance measure, we have reported summarized results in terms of minimum, average, and the maximum value of each ensemble method.

Table 3.3 Experimental procedure for homogeneous ensemble methods

Input:	D: A set of twenty-eight software fault datasets augmented with object-oriented software metrics and fault information, D= {D_1, D_2, …, D_{28}}
	M: A set of five ensemble methods, M = {Bagging, Boosting, Rotation Forest, Random Subspace, Stacking}
	L: A set of three base learners, L = {Linear regression, Multilayer perceptron, Decision tree regression}
Output:	Performance of ensemble methods in terms of mean absolute error, means relative error, Pred(0.30) (prediction at level 0.30)

Begin:

1.   for each software fault dataset $d \in D$

2.   for each ensemble method $m \in M$

3.   for each base learner $l \in L$

4.   apply technique m with l as base learner over d and perform 10-fold cross- validation

5.   record the predicted value of number of faults for each software module

6.   end for

7.   end for

8.   end for

9.   Calculate the error in terms of mean absolute error and mean relative error using the value of predicted number of faults and actual number of faults for the given software modules.

10.   Calculate pred(0.30) values using the values of mean relative errors.

End

Table 3.4 Results of experiment for group-1 datasets (datasets have less than 10% of faulty modules, 5 datasets)

Technique	Base learner	MAE			MRE		
		Min	Avg.	Max	Min	Avg.	Max
Bagging	DTR	0.02	0.10	0.16	0.011	0.05	0.08
	LR	0.03	0.10	0.173	0.02	0.055	0.088
	MLP	0.044	0.12	0.18	0.03	0.076	0.114
Boosting	DTR	0.02	0.10	0.171	0.01	0.055	0.092
	LR	0.03	0.10	0.172	0.017	0.056	0.095
	MLP	0.05	0.17	0.319	0.03	0.125	0.239
Random subspace	DTR	0.02	0.100	0.163	0.0115	0.050	0.084
	LR	0.026	0.100	0.168	0.013	0.050	0.828
	MLP	0.028	0.190	0.314	0.016	0.143	0.235
Rotation forest	DTR	0.02	0.099	0.161	0.0115	0.050	0.084
	LR	0.030	0.104	0.173	0.017	0.055	0.089
	MLP	0.060	0.1773	0.247	0.048	0.127	0.235
Stacking	DTR	0.030	0.104	0.169	0.017	0.055	0.08
	LR	0.030	0.101	0.165	0.017	0.052	0.0839
	MLP	0.026	0.1313	0.323	0.013	0.081	0.244

Table 3.5 Results of experiment for group-2 datasets (datasets have faulty modules between 10 and 20%, 12 datasets)

Technique	Base learner	MAE			MRE		
		Min	Avg.	Max	Min	Avg.	Max
Bagging	DTR	0.124	0.305	0.663	0.073	0.161	0.326
	LR	0.146	0.325	0.708	0.077	0.1779	0.389
	MLP	0.1752	0.342	0.622	0.084	0.192	0.320
Boosting	DTR	0.152	0.322	0.692	0.086	0.181	0.363
	LR	0.143	0.332	0.731	0.076	0.186	0.414
	MLP	0.110	0.426	1.02	0.084	0.279	0.832
Random subspace	DTR	0.13	0.300	0.640	0.072	0.1553	0.325
	LR	0.133	0.3151	0.6893	0.074	0.1668	0.374
	MLP	0.143	0.4065	1.017	0.081	0.252	0.821
Rotation forest	DTR	0.124	0.301	0.632	0.066	0.158	0.319
	LR	0.149	0.328	0.719	0.075	0.182	0.405
	MLP	0.171	0.424	1.019	0.082	0.268	0.825
Stacking	DTR	0.121	0.3023	0.616	0.061	0.152	0.299
	LR	0.12	0.306	0.654	0.06	0.155	0.336
	MLP	0.124	0.464	1.23	0.066	0.309	0.906

Table 3.6 Results of experiment for group-3 datasets (datasets have faulty modules between 20 and 30%, 3 datasets)

Technique	Base learner	MAE			MRE		
		Min	Avg.	Max	Min	Avg.	Max
Bagging	DTR	0.3919	0.564	0.679	0.21	0.294	0.347
	LR	0.414	0.623	0.787	0.233	0.362	0.496
	MLP	0.489	0.655	0.762	0.287	0.360	0.432
Boosting	DTR	0.405	0.641	0.761	0.204	0.336	0.427
	LR	0.416	0.632	0.764	0.236	0.363	0.482
	MLP	0.684	0.841	1.003	0.448	0.529	0.636
Random subspace	DTR	0.381	0.577	0.6993	0.199	0.292	0.349
	LR	0.420	0.631	0.761	0.240	0.360	0.449
	MLP	0.518	0.669	0.784	0.324	0.374	0.440
Rotation forest	DTR	0.377	0.533	0.656	0.202	0.278	0.341
	LR	0.481	0.610	0.722	0.240	0.346	0.440
	MLP	0.626	0.815	0.923	0.398	0.494	0.552
Stacking	DTR	0.417	0.568	0.676	0.223	0.266	0.314
	LR	0.405	0.626	0.777	0.222	0.331	0.415
	MLP	0.5006	0.768	0.983	0.319	0.467	0.575

Table 3.7 Results of experiment for group-4 datasets (datasets have faulty modules 30% or more, 8 datasets)

Technique	Base learner	MAE			MRE		
		Min	Avg.	Max	Min	Avg.	Max
Bagging	DTR	0.275	0.803	1.70	0.10	0.373	0.62
	LR	0.319	0.849	1.833	0.115	0.407	0.625
	MLP	0.312	0.924	2.11	0.117	0.427	0.6703
Boosting	DTR	0.303	0.836	1.81	0.115	0.390	0.615
	LR	0.331	0.865	1.88	0.119	0.413	0.635
	MLP	0.349	1.08	2.12	0.126	0.527	0.832
Random subspace	DTR	0.266	0.815	1.69	0.09	0.384	0.635
	LR	0.312	0.861	1.79	0.109	0.413	0.633
	MLP	0.305	1.09	2.03	0.104	0.511	0.821
Rotation forest	DTR	0.267	0.812	1.72	0.098	0.3773	0.619
	LR	0.321	0.859	1.86	0.115	0.408	0.621
	MLP	0.295	1.04	2.06	0.108	0.523	0.825
Stacking	DTR	0.297	0.851	1.87	0.109	0.450	0.766
	LR	0.286	0.858	1.88	0.103	0.426	0.669
	MLP	0.317	0.107	2.54	0.108	0.503	0.868

3.3.1 Results of Group-1 for MAE and MRE

This group included fault datasets have less than 10% of the faulty software modules.
Five fault datasets have been fallen into this group. Results for this group in terms
of MAE and MRE are given in Table 3.4. The observations based on Table 3.4 are
summarized below.

- With respect to the MAE measure, minimum error value varies between 0.02 and
  0.06, and maximum error value varies between 0.16 and 0.323. The average error
  value varies between 0.09 and 0.19. All ensemble methods produced values below
  0.30. The best performance is produced by bagging with DTR as a base learning
  technique. Random subspace and rotation forest with DTR as a base learner produced the results comparable to the bagging. Other ensemble methods are also
  produced comparable results. Stacking with MLP as a base learner and boosting with MLP as a base learner performed relatively poor for MAE performance
  measure.
- With respect to the MRE measure, minimum error value varies between 0.01 and
  0.03, and maximum error value varies between 0.08 and 0.244. The average error
  value varies between 0.05 and 0.14. All ensemble methods produced values below
  0.25. The best performance is produced by bagging with DTR as a base learning
  technique. Random subspace and rotation forest with DTR as base learner produced the similar results as of bagging. Other ensemble methods are also produced
  comparable results. Stacking with MLP as a base learner and random subspace
  with MLP as a base learner performed relatively poor for MRE performance measure.
- Overall, bagging, random subspace, and rotation forest have performed relatively
  better compared to other used ensemble methods for both the performance measures. DTR as a base learner performed the best.

3.3.2 Results of Group-2 for MAE and MRE

This group included fault datasets have faulty software modules between 10 and
20%. Twelve fault datasets have been fallen into this group. Results for this group in
terms of MAE and MRE are given in Table 3.5. The observations based on Table 3.5
are summarized below.

- In terms of MAE measure, minimum error value varies between 0.11 and 0.172
  and maximum error value varies between 0.62 and 1.23. The average error value
  varies between 0.30 and 0.46. Most of the ensemble methods produced values
  below 0.65. The best performance is produced by rotation forest with DTR as a
  base learning technique. Random subspace and bagging with DTR as a base learner
  produced the results comparable to the rotation forest. Other ensemble methods are
  also produced comparable results. Stacking with MLP as a base learner performed
  relatively poor for MAE performance measure.

- With respect to the MRE measure, minimum error value varies between 0.06 and 0.084, and maximum error value varies between 0.319 and 0.906. The average error value varies between 0.26 and 0.309. Most of the ensemble methods produced values below 0.40. The best performance is produced by rotation forest with DTR as a base learning technique. Random subspace and bagging with DTR as a base learner produced the results comparable to the rotation forest. Other ensemble methods are also produced comparable results. Stacking with MLP as a base learner performed relatively poor for MRE performance measure.
- Overall, rotation forest, bagging, and random subspace have performed relatively better compared to other used ensemble methods for both the performance measures. DTR as a base learner performed the best.

3.3.3 Results of Group-3 for MAE and MRE

Group-3 included fault datasets have faulty software modules between 20 and 30%. Three fault datasets have been fallen into this group. Results for this group in terms of MAE and MRE are given in Table 3.6. The observations based on Table 3.6 are summarized below.

- For MAE measure, minimum error value varies between 0.377 and 0.68 and maximum error value varies between 0.656 and 1.03. The average error value varies between 0.53 and 0.81. Most of the ensemble methods produced values below 0.70. Rotation forest with DTR as a base learner produced the best performance. Random subspace and bagging with DTR as a base learner produced the results comparable to the rotation forest. Boosting and stacking with MLP as a base learner performed relatively poor for MAE performance measure.
- For MRE measure, minimum error value varies between 0.19 and 0.39, and maximum error value varies between 0.34 and 0.63. The average error value varies between 0.27 and 0.52. Most of the ensemble methods produced values below 0.40. Random subspace and rotation forest with DTR as a base learner produced the best results. Bagging with DTR as a base learner produced the results comparable to the rotation forest. Other ensemble methods are also produced comparable results. Boosting and stacking with MLP as a base learner performed relatively poor for MRE performance measure.
- Overall, rotation forest, random subspace and bagging have occupied top positions and performed relatively better compared to other used ensemble methods for both the performance measures. DTR as a base learner performed the best.

3.3.4   Results of Group-4 for MAE and MRE

Group-4 included fault datasets have faulty software modules 30% or more. Eight
fault datasets have been fallen into this group. Results for this group in terms of MAE
and MRE are given in Table 3.7. The observations based on Table 3.7 are summarized
below.

- With respect to MAE measure, minimum error value varies between 0.26 and 0.349
  and maximum error value varies between 1.69 and 2.54. The average error value
  varies between 0.80 and 1.09. Most of the ensemble methods produced relatively
  higher values for MAE. Random subspace with DTR as a base learner produced
  the best performance. Rotation forest and bagging with DTR as a base learner
  produced the results comparable to the rotation forest. Stacking and boosting with
  MLP as a base learner performed relatively poor for MAE performance measure.
- With respect to MRE measure, minimum error value varies between 0.09 and 0.11,
  and maximum error value varies between 0.619 and 0.86. The average error value
  varies between 0.37 and 0.52. Most of the ensemble methods produced values
  below 0.40. Random subspace and rotation forest with DTR as a base learner
  produced the best results. Bagging with DTR as base learner produced the results
  comparable to the rotation forest. Boosting and stacking with MLP as a base learner
  performed relatively poor for MRE performance measure.
- Overall, rotation forest, random subspace and bagging have occupied top positions
  and performed relatively better compared to other used ensemble methods for both
  the performance measures. DTR as a base learner performed the best.

These results showed that generally, homogeneous ensemble methods produced
better performance, when number of faulty modules in software systems are low
(below 20%). As percentage of faulty modules increase, performance of ensemble
methods decreases. This trend has been follows by most of the homogeneous ensemble methods. Overall, bagging, rotation forest, and random subspace performed better compared to other used ensemble methods, and boosting and stacking produced
relatively poor performance.

3.3.5   Results of Pred(0.30) for All Groups of Fault Datasets

Results of pred(0.30) performance measure for all the used homogeneous ensemble
methods have been reported in Tables 3.8, 3.9, 3.10 and 3.11. Each table shows
summarized results in terms of minimum, median, and maximum of one group of
datasets. The following observations have been drawn from these tables:

- For group-1 fault datasets, minimum value varies between 72.2 and 88.8%, maximum value varies between 95.9 and 97.7%. Median value varies between 81.99
  and 89.86%. Bagging with DTR as a base learner performed the best followed
  by random subspace and rotation forest with DTR as a base learner. Most of the

Table 3.8 Pred(0.30) results of experiment for group-1 datasets (in percentage)

Technique	Base learner	Pred(0.30)		
		Min	Median	Max
Bagging	DTR	88.38	88.80	97.76
	LR	87.65	89.40	97.16
	MLP	86.08	89.26	95.94
Boosting	DTR	87.31	89.25	97.56
	LR	87.66	89.56	97.56
	MLP	73.08	87.54	96.75
Random subspace	DTR	88.08	89.71	97.76
	LR	88.06	89.86	97.56
	MLP	73.29	81.99	97.36
Rotation forest	DTR	85.68	89.86	97.76
	LR	87.60	89.25	97.56
	MLP	75.58	87.66	95.33
Stacking	DTR	88.03	89.10	97.16
	LR	88.32	89.71	97.16
	MLP	72.77	89.71	97.56

Table 3.9 Pred(0.30) results of experiment for group-2 datasets (in percentage)

Technique	Base learner	Pred(0.30)		
		Min	Median	Max
Bagging	DTR	66.25	81.84	88.57
	LR	63.66	81.51	87.27
	MLP	64.39	79.86	86.78
Boosting	DTR	56.82	81.16	86.84
	LR	50.22	80.89	87.83
	MLP	53.52	79.74	86.84
Random subspace	DTR	64.09	82.11	88.25
	LR	55.28	80.82	87.93
	MLP	41.58	82.11	87.55
Rotation forest	DTR	64.09	81.44	88.57
	LR	52.42	81.03	87.45
	MLP	52.64	78.88	87.04
Stacking	DTR	48.23	81.84	88.57
	LR	45.37	82.05	88.57
	MLP	31.93	72.71	88.25

Table 3.10 Pred(0.30) results of experiment for group-3 datasets (in percentage)

Technique	Base learner	Pred(0.30)		
		Min	Median	Max
Bagging	DTR	65.14	65.81	75.06
	LR	59.28	63.89	73.72
	MLP	67.09	68.40	70.50
Boosting	DTR	64.53	65.79	74.53
	LR	61.88	63.25	73.05
	MLP	57.00	58.47	60.18
Random subspace	DTR	65.79	69.64	75.20
	LR	60.91	61.98	71.04
	MLP	59.28	62.33	68.69
Rotation forest	DTR	65.47	69.32	75.73
	LR	61.88	64.21	73.05
	MLP	54.39	59.11	62.30
Stacking	DTR	67.42	71.56	73.99
	LR	60.70	60.91	73.59
	MLP	47.60	49.51	63.40

Table 3.11 Pred(0.30) results of experiment for group-4 datasets (in percentage)

Technique	Base learner	Pred(0.30)		
		Min	Median	Max
Bagging	DTR	33.13	55.43	80.0
	LR	37.24	51.29	76.65
	MLP	34.46	50.89	79.61
Boosting	DTR	32.55	47.64	79.08
	LR	37.24	44.90	76.53
	MLP	28.90	48.74	79.76
Random subspace	DTR	31.37	49.39	79.39
	LR	33.72	44.06	77.26
	MLP	29.03	41.64	66.69
Rotation forest	DTR	33.13	51.07	78.75
	LR	36.65	44.69	76.77
	MLP	30.10	43.36	66.63
Stacking	DTR	29.03	45.24	78.09
	LR	31.08	45.04	67.48
	MLP	24.61	39.87	61.35

ensemble methods achieved values greater than 80% with the exception in the case of stacking and boosting with MLP as a base learner.

- For group-2 fault datasets, minimum value varies between 31.93 and 66.25%, maximum value varies between 86.8 and 88.7%. Median value varies between 72.7 and 82.11%. Bagging with DTR as base learner performed the best followed by random subspace and rotation forest with DTR as a base learner. Most of the ensemble methods achieved values greater than 70% with the exception in the case of stacking with MLP as a base learner.

- With respect to group-3 fault datasets, minimum value varies between 47.6 and 67.42%, maximum value varies between 63.09 and 75.05%. Median value varies between 49.51 and 71.56%. Stacking with DTR as a base learner performed the best followed by bagging with DTR as a base learner. Most of the ensemble methods achieved values greater than 70% with the exception in the case of stacking and boosting with MLP as a base learner.

- For group-4 fault datasets, minimum value varies between 24.61 and 37.24%, maximum value varies between 61.35 and 80%. Median value varies between 39.8 and 49.39%. Bagging and boosting with LR as a base learner performed the best followed by rotation forest with LR as a base learner. Most of the ensemble methods achieved values greater than 40% with the exception in the case of stacking with MLP as a base learner.

- Overall, it has found that except for group-4 fault datasets, homogeneous ensemble methods performed significantly accurate for pred(0.30) performance measure. For most of the cases, values are above 70% showing the better performance of ensemble methods.

3.4 Summary

In the last few years, the use of homogeneous ensemble methods for building software fault prediction models is increased significantly. However, most of the studies available in the literature regarding homogeneous ensemble methods are not articulated enough to draw any generalized arguments. The earlier evaluation of these methods suffered from the various factors such as the complexity of techniques used source fault datasets, and used performance evaluation measures, etc. In the presented work, we built and evaluated five different homogeneous ensemble methods for the number of faults prediction. Some of the used ensemble methods already evaluated for software fault prediction and some other ensemble methods are novel in the presented study, and others are the variants of the already available techniques. For each method, we used three different learning techniques as base learners. Therefore, total fifteen fault prediction models have built for each fault dataset. The experimental analysis was performed for 28 software fault datasets grouped into four different groups based on the percentage of faulty modules in the datasets. Experimental results showed that used homogeneous ensemble methods produced a better performance when number of faulty modules in software systems is low (below 20%). As the percentage of faulty modules increase, the performance of ensemble methods decreases. Overall, rotation forest, bagging, and random subspace occupied the top three positions and performed better as compared to other used ensemble methods. Results of the presented study could be useful to the researchers and software practitioners to select an appropriate ensemble method for the prediction of number of faults in the early phases of the software development.

References

1. Amasaki, S.: Cross-version defect prediction using cross-project defect prediction approaches: does it work? In: Proceedings of the 14th International Conference on Predictive Models and Data Analytics in Software Engineering, pp. 32–41 (2018)
2. Boetticher, G.: The PROMISE repository of empirical software engineering data. http://promisedata.org/repository (2007)
3. D'Ambros, M., Lanza, M., Robbes, R.: An extensive comparison of bug prediction approaches. In: Proceedings of 7th IEEE Working Conference on Mining Software Repositories (MSR), pp. 31–41 (2010)
4. Elish, M.O., Aljamaan, H., Ahmad, I.: Three empirical studies on predicting software maintainability using ensemble methods. Soft Comput. **19**(9), 1–14 (2015)
5. Elish, M.O., Al-Yafei, A.H., Al-Mulhem, M.: Empirical comparison of three metrics suites for fault prediction in packages of object-oriented systems: a case study of eclipse. Adv. Eng. Softw. **42**(10), 852–859 (2011)
6. Holmes, G., Donkin, A., Witten, I.H.: Weka: A machine learning workbench. In: Proceedings of the 2nd Australian and New Zealand Conference on Intelligent Information Systems, pp. 357–361 (1994)
7. Jureczko, M., Madeyski, L.: Towards identifying software project clusters with regard to defect prediction. In: Proceedings of the 6th International Conference on Predictive Models in Software Engineering, p. 9 (2010)
8. Kumar, S., Rathore, S.S: Software Fault Prediction a Road Map. Springer Brief in Computer Science, 1st edn, pp. 1–72. Springer (2018)
9. Mendes-Moreira, J., Soares, C., Jorge, A.M., Sousa, J.F.D.: Ensemble approaches for regression: A survey. ACM Comput. Surv. (CSUR) **45**(1), 10 (2012)
10. Rathore, S.S., Kumar, S.: An empirical study of some software fault prediction techniques for the number of faults prediction. Soft. Comput. **21**(24), 7417–7434 (2017)
11. Rathore, S.S., Kumar, S.: Ensemble methods for the prediction of number of faults: a study on eclipse project. In 11th International Conference on Industrial and Information Systems (ICIIS), pp. 540–545 (2016)
12. Shatnawi, R., Li, W.: The effectiveness of software metrics in identifying error-prone classes in post-release software evolution process. J. Syst. Softw. **81**(11), 1868–1882 (2008)
13. Zhu, X., He, Y., Cheng, L., Jia, X., Zhu L.: Software change-proneness prediction through combination of bagging and resampling methods. J. Softw.: Evol. Process., e2111 (2011)

Chapter 4
Linear Rule Based Ensemble Methods for the Prediction of Number of Faults

Software fault prediction models are highly influenced by the use of learning techniques and characteristics of fault datasets. Previous studies related to the software fault prediction showed that the use of individual learning techniques seems incompetent to handle this problem [4, 6, 9, 12, 14]. However, the use of multiple learning technique, where each technique is proficient for a subpart of fault dataset and combining all such learning techniques decisions can improve the overall prediction performance. This raises the need for using multiple learning techniques for predicting faults in a given software project. One such approach (homogeneous ensemble methods) has been presented in the previous chapter. The analysis of various homogeneous ensemble methods presented in Chap. 3 shows that an improved fault prediction performance could be achieved by combining the decision of multiple learning models for the prediction of a number of faults. Some other related studies also showed that the use of multiple learning techniques can be helpful in getting better performance as compared to the individual learning technique [5].

Another way is to use multiple learning techniques and generate intermediate prediction models corresponding to each learning techniques. Final prediction is based on the combine decision of all intermediate learning models [1]. In this chapter, we present different linear heterogeneous ensemble methods for the prediction of number of faults in the software projects.

4.1 Linear Rule Based Heterogeneous Ensemble Methods

In homogeneous ensemble methods, we harness the prediction capability of only one learning technique by generating multiple learning models from it. This type of ensemble methods may suffer from the lack of diversity in base learners. Moreover, error in the learning of prediction technique can propagate in all generated interme- diate prediction models. Therefore, it might be better to use more than one learning techniques since different techniques can perform best locally and combining their

S. S. Rathore and S. Kumar, *Fault Prediction Modeling for the Prediction of Number of Software Faults*, SpringerBriefs in Computer Science, https://doi.org/10.1007/978-981-13-7131-8_4

outputs can help in achieving overall better prediction [10, 20]. Additionally, using more than one learning techniques increase the generalization of prediction results.

In heterogeneous ensemble methods, more than one learning techniques are used to build the ensemble methods. In these ensemble methods, learning is twofolds. In the first fold, different base learners are generated by applying learning techniques over the training dataset. In second fold, generated models are combined for the ensemble using various combination methods [13]. Use of diverse learning techniques decreases variance in the prediction and leads to the generalization error to be lesser than the generalization error of individual learning technique [3, 7]. We have used linear rule based heterogeneous ensemble methods, where outputs of base learners are combined in a linear form respected to their contribution in the occurring of the final output [18].

4.2   Evaluation of Linear Rule Based Heterogeneous Ensemble Methods

We performed an experimental analysis and evaluated the performance of heterogeneous ensemble methods for the prediction of number of faults.

The elements of experimental analysis are described in the upcoming subsections.

4.2.1 Software Fault Datasets

We have used software fault datasets available in the PROMISE data repository to build and evaluate heterogeneous ensemble methods base fault prediction models [2, 19]. We have used same 28 software fault datasets as described in the Chap. 3 Sect. 3.2.1. All the used fault datasets have same 20 object-oriented software metrics (independent variables) and number of faults information as dependent variable. A detailed description of these datasets is given in Chap. 3.

4.2.2 Experimental Setup

As described in the Chap. 3, we have categorized used software fault datasets into four different groups based on the percentage of faulty modules in given fault datasets. Subsequently, we built and evaluated prediction models for each group of fault datasets. Details about different groups of software fault datasets are given in Table 3.2. Group-1 contains all the fault datasets having a percentage of faulty software modules below 10%. Fault datasets have faulty software modules between 10 and 20% categorized into group-2. Fault datasets have faulty software modules between 20 and 30% categorized into group-3. Group-4 contains all the fault datasets have 30% or more faulty software modules.

4.2.3 Experimental Procedure

The experimental procedure adopted for building and evaluating ensemble methods based fault prediction models is given in Table 4.1. The experimental procedure is adopted from the work presented by Rathore and Kumar [17].

Partition the Fault Dataset

We partitioned original fault dataset into three disjoint subsets as training dataset (60% of original dataset), validation dataset (20% of original dataset), and testing dataset (20% of original dataset). The dataset partitions are generated by using stratification process, in which the total population is partitioned into nonoverlapping partitions. Each partition receives proper representation of the population distribution [16]. The advantage of using stratification process is that it keeps the data distribution in each partition close to that in the entire population.

Validation Phase

The working of heterogeneous ensemble methods involves the use of an integration function. We have used validation dataset to derive integration function, which combines outputs of the base learning techniques for the ensemble. The use of separate validation dataset ensures that base learning techniques achieve generalization and are not overfit for training dataset. Each base learning technique is applied for validation dataset and their results are stored. Afterwards, an integration function is derived based on the performance of base learning techniques for the validation dataset. This integration function is further used to combine the final predictions in the testing phase.

Testing Phase

Testing dataset is used for final unbiased evaluation of ensemble methods. After the training phase and validation phase, each trained learning technique is applied to the testing dataset. For each testing dataset module, each base learning technique predicts a potential number of faults. Next a linear combination rule (ERWT or LRWT) is used to combine the outputs of the base learning techniques for the ensemble.

Combination Rules to Integrate the Outputs of the Learning Techniques for Ensemble Method

In this work, we have used linear combination rules, namely error rate based and linear regression based to combine the outputs of base learning techniques for the ensemble. In the first rule mean relative error (MRE) is used to determine weights of base learning techniques in the ensemble [15]. Weights are inversely proportional to the MRE value, lower the MRE value, higher the weight. In second rule linear regression (LR) analysis is used to determine weights of base learning techniques in the ensemble [11]. A linear regression model is fit between predicted values of the faults by learning techniques and corresponding actual values of faults for the validation dataset, which shows the contributions of base learning techniques. A detailed description of these combination rules is given in Chap. 2, Sect. 2.2.

Table 4.1 Experimental procedure for linear rule based heterogeneous ensemble methods

---

Input: D: A set of twenty-eight software fault datasets augmented with object-oriented software metrics and fault information, D = {D_1, D_2, ..., D_{28}}

S: A set of L base learning techniques S= {s_1,...,s_L},//Here, Base learning techniques ={ Linear regression, Multilayer perceptron, Decision tree regression}

Preprocessing:

Split the whole fault dataset into three parts as training dataset, validation dataset, and testing dataset.

Training dataset TR = tr_1,...,tr_N containing N modules
Validation dataset V = v_1,...,v_V containing V modules

Testing dataset TE = te_1,...,te_R containing R modules

Begin:

1. for each learning techniques s_j ϵ S, j = 1,...,L

2.   Train s_j over TR

3. end for

4. for each module in validation dataset $v_i \epsilon$ V, i=1,...,V

5.   Apply each learning technique in S over v_i

6.   Derive an integration function $Y_{int}(x)$ // $Y_{int}(x)$ is used to combine the predictions of the learning techniques for the ensemble

7. end for

8. for each module in testing dataset $te_i \epsilon$ TE, i=1,...,R

9.   Apply each learning technique in S over te_i

10.   Store the output values o_{ij} for the module te_i after applying each learning techniques s_1,...,s_L in Out_te_i //Where, O_{ij} is the predicted number of faults for te_i using s_j , Out_te_i = {O_{i1},...,O_{iL} } is a row in i×j matrix , i=1,...,R; j=1,..,L

11. end for

12.   Final Prediction = $Y_{int}($Out_t_{1e}, Out_te_2,..., Out_$te_R)$

End

4.2.4   Tools and Techniques Used for Experiment

We have used *RemovePercentage*[1] filter to partition the original fault dataset into training dataset, validation dataset, and testing dataset. The implementation of this filter is available in the Weka machine learning tool [8]. We have used Weka implementation of base learning techniques used in the ensemble methods. To assess the performance of built fault prediction models, we have used mean absolute error (MAE), mean relative error (MRE), and pred(0.30) performance measures.

4.3   Results and Discussion

Using the experimental procedure discussed in Table 4.1, we have built linear rule based ensemble methods for the prediction of number of faults in the software systems. We grouped results into four different groups as identified in Table 3.2 and reported results in terms of mean absolute error (MAE) and mean relative error (MRE). Tables 4.2, 4.3, 4.4, and 4.5 show the results of experimental analysis. Each table is corresponding to one group of software fault datasets and shows results of MAE and MRE. For each performance measure, we have reported summarized results in terms of minimum, average, and maximum value of each ensemble method.

4.3.1   Results of Group-1 for MAE and MRE

Table 4.2 shows the results in terms of MAE and MRE for five group-1 fault datasets have less than 10% faulty software modules. The observations based on Table 4.2 are summarized below.

Table 4.2 Results of experiment for group-1 datasets (datasets have less than 10% of faulty modules, 5 datasets)

Technique	MAE			MRE		
	Min	Avg.	Max	Min	Avg.	Max
Basic ensemble method	0.05	0.114	0.1537	0.0219	0.061	0.0754
Best in training ensemble method	0.05	0.104	0.1542	0.021	0.050	0.0754
Error rate based ensemble method	0.050	0.114	0.1537	0.0219	0.0613	0.0754
Linear regression based ensemble method	0.058	0.100	0.1514	0.0294	0.043	0.066

---

[1]Remove Percentage filter, http://weka.sourceforge.net/doc.dev/weka/filters/unsupervised/instance/RemovePercentage.html.

Table 4.3 Results of experiment for group-2 datasets (Datasets have faulty modules between 10 and 20%, 12 datasets)

Technique	MAE			MRE		
	Min	Avg.	Max	Min	Avg.	Max
Basic ensemble method	0.098	0.329	0.6057	0.0622	0.192	0.4167
Best in training ensemble Method	0.0952	0.315	0.6114	0.0423	0.176	0.358
Error rate based ensemble method	0.0986	0.326	0.595	0.0622	0.188	0.3883
Linear regression based ensemble method	0.1747	0.409	1.41	0.0825	0.268	1.25

Table 4.4 Results of experiment for group-3 datasets (datasets have faulty modules between 20 and 30%, 3 datasets)

Technique	MAE			MRE		
	Min	Avg.	Max	Min	Avg.	Max
Basic ensemble method	0.39	0.484	0.539	0.206	0.256	0.305
Best in training ensemble method	0.3826	0.541	0.639	0.235	0.296	0.405
Error rate based ensemble method	0.396	0.525	0.639	0.206	0.281	0.377
Linear regression based ensemble method	0.362	0.660	0.983	0.236	0.369	0.63

Table 4.5 Results of experiment for group-4 datasets (datasets have 30% or more faulty modules, 8 datasets)

Technique	MAE			MRE		
	Min	Avg.	Max	Min	Avg.	Max
Basic ensemble method	0.258	0.944	2.16	0.0832	0.550	1.5
Best in training ensemble method	0.346	0.930	2.15	0.117	0.5009	1.39
Error rate based ensemble method	0.2582	0.901	2.15	0.097	0.514	1.26
Linear regression based ensemble method	0.269	0.920	2.36	0.087	0.500	1.176

- With respect to the MAE measure, minimum error value varies between 0.05 and 0.058, and maximum error value varies between 0.152 and 0.154. The average error value varies between 0.10 and 0.114. All ensemble methods produced values below 0.154. The best performance is produced by linear regression based ensemble method and best in training ensemble method. Other ensemble methods also produced comparable results.
- With respect to the MRE measure, minimum error value varies between 0.021 and 0.029, and maximum error value varies between 0.066 and 0.0754. The average error value varies between 0.043 and 0.061. All ensemble methods produced values below 0.075. The best performance is produced by linear regression based ensemble method. Other ensemble methods also produced comparable results.

- Overall, all ensemble methods produced better prediction performance for both the performance measures and linear regression based ensemble method performed the best.

4.3.2   Results of Group-2 for MAE and MRE

Table 4.3 shows the results in terms of MAE and MRE for 12 group-2 fault datasets having faulty software module between 10 and 20%. The observations based on Table 4.3 are summarized below.

- In terms of MAE measure, minimum error value varies between 0.095 and 0.174 and maximum error value varies between 0.60 and 1.41. The average error value varies between 0.31 and 0.40. Most of the ensemble methods produced values below 0.61. The best performance is produced by best in training ensemble method and error rate based ensemble method. Other ensemble methods also produced comparable results.
- With respect to the MRE measure, minimum error value varies between 0.04 and 0.08, and maximum error value varies between 0.319 and 1.25. The average error value varies between 0.17 and 0.26. Most of the ensemble methods produced values below 0.40. The best performance is produced by best in training ensemble method. Other ensemble methods also produced comparable results.
- Overall, best in training ensemble method and error rate based ensemble method performed relatively better compared to other used ensemble methods for both the performance measures.

4.3.3   Results of Group-3 for MAE and MRE

Table 4.4 shows the results in terms of MAE and MRE for three group-3 fault datasets have faulty software modules between 20 and 30%. The observations based on Table 4.4 are summarized below.

- For MAE measure, minimum error value varies between 0.36 and 0.396 and maximum error value varies between 0.539 and 0.983. The average error value varies between 0.484 and 0.66. Most of the ensemble methods produced values below 0.50. Basic ensemble method produced better results compared to other ensemble methods.
- For MRE measure, minimum error value varies between 0.206 and 0.235, and maximum error value varies between 0.30 and 0.63. The average error value varies between 0.256 and 0.369. Most of the ensemble methods produced values below 0.40. Basic ensemble method produced better results compared to other ensemble methods. Other ensemble methods also produced comparable results.

- Overall, basic ensemble method produced better results compared to other ensemble methods performed relatively better compared to other used ensemble methods for both the performance measures.

4.3.4   Results of Group-4 for MAE and MRE

Group-4 included fault datasets have faulty software modules 30% or more. Eight fault datasets have been fallen into this group. Summarized results for this group in terms of MAE and MRE are given in Table 4.5. The observations based on the table are summarized below.

- With respect to MAE measure, minimum error value varies between 0.258 and 0.346 and maximum error value varies between 2.15 and 2.16. The average error value varies between 0.901 and 0.944. Most of the ensemble methods produced relatively higher values for MAE. Error rate based ensemble method produced the best performance.
- With respect to MRE measure, minimum error value varies between 0.08 and 0.11, and maximum error value varies between 1.17 and 1.5. The average error value varies between 0.50 and 0.55. Most of the ensemble methods produced average values below 0.55. Linear regression based ensemble method produced the best results.
- Overall, basic ensemble method, linear regression based ensemble method, and error rate based ensemble method have occupied top positions and performed relatively better compared. ʼ

From the results, it has been observed that generally, linear rule based heterogeneous ensemble methods produced better performance when number of faulty modules in software systems are low (below 20%). As percentage of faulty modules increases, the performance of ensemble methods decreases. This trend has been followed by most of the used ensemble methods. However, low variation among the performance of used ensemble methods has been found. It shows more stable performance of heterogeneous ensemble methods with compared to homogeneous ensemble method.

4.3.5   Results of Pred(0.30) for All Groups of Fault Datasets

Tables 4.6, 4.7, 4.8 and 4.9 show results of pred(0.30) performance measure for all the used linear rule based heterogeneous ensemble methods. The results are summarized in terms of minimum, median, and maximum of one group of datasets in each table. Following observations have been drawn from these tables as discussed below.

- For group-1 fault datasets, minimum value varies between 89.0 and 89.3%, maximum value varies between 95.6 and 95.9%. Median value varies between 89.7 and

Table 4.6 Pred(0.30) results of experiment for group-1 datasets (in percentage)

Technique	Pred(0.30)		
	Min	Median	Max
Basic ensemble method	89.0	89.70	95.6
Best in training Ensemble Method	89.2	90.15	95.86
Error rate based ensemble method	89.0	89.71	95.90
Linear regression based ensemble method	89.30	91.80	95.90

Table 4.7 Pred(0.30) results of experiment for group-2 datasets (in percentage)

Technique	Pred(0.30)		
	Min	Median	Max
Basic ensemble method	57.90	80.70	94.30
Best in training ensemble method	64.70	78.60	92.00
Error rate based ensemble method	56.80	80.70	94.30
Linear regression based ensemble method	57.00	78.60	92.00

Table 4.8 Pred(0.30) results of experiment for group-3 datasets (in percentage)

Technique	Pred(0.30)		
	Min	Median	Max
Basic ensemble method	72.00	71.00	73.00
Best in training ensemble method	69.80	70.40	71.80
Error rate based ensemble method	70.40	71.80	73.00
Linear regression based ensemble method	40.90	66.70	72.40

Table 4.9 Pred(0.30) results of experiment for group-4 datasets (in percentage)

Technique	Pred(0.30)		
	Min	Median	Max
Basic ensemble method	28.90	54.50	82.40
Best in training ensemble method	29.40	53.30	79.10
Error rate based ensemble method	29.40	54.50	80.70
Linear regression based ensemble method	26.40	49.30	79.60

91.8%. Linear regression based ensemble method performed the best followed by best in training ensemble method. All ensemble methods achieved values greater than 89%.

- For group-2 fault datasets, minimum value varies between 56.8 and 64.7%, maximum value varies between 92.0 and 94.3%. Median value varies between 78.6 and 80.7%. Most of the ensemble methods achieved median values greater than 78%.
- With respect to group-3 fault datasets, minimum value varies between 40.9 and 72%, maximum value varies between 71.8 and 73%. Median value varies between 66.7 and 71.8%. Basic ensemble method performed the best followed by error rate based ensemble method. Most of the ensemble methods achieved median values greater than 70%.
- For group-4 fault datasets, minimum value varies between 26.4 and 29.4%, maximum value varies between 79.6 and 82.4%. Median value varies between 49.3 and 54.5% error rate based ensemble method performed the best followed by best in training ensemble method. Most of the ensemble methods achieved median values greater than 53% with the exception in the case of linear regression based ensemble method.
- Overall, it has found that for all group of fault datasets, linear rule based ensemble methods performed significantly accurate for pred(0.30) performance measure. For most of the cases, median values are above 70% showing the better performance of ensemble methods.

4.4   Summary

The work presented in this chapter focused on the evaluation of linear rule based heterogeneous ensemble methods for the prediction of number of faults. Presented ensemble methods utilized the capabilities of multiple learning techniques and combined them in a linear form to improve the overall performance of fault prediction. In the present study, we explored the use of four different linear rule based ensemble methods and evaluated the performance of used methods through an experimental analysis for 28 software fault datasets. Performance of built prediction models has been assessed using MAE, MRE, and pred(0.30) performance evaluation measures. From results, it has been observed that generally, linear rule based heterogeneous ensemble methods produced better performance, when a number of faulty modules in software systems are low (below 20%). This trend has been follows by most of the used ensemble methods. Moreover, a low variation among the performance of used ensemble methods has been found. It shows more stable performance of heterogeneous ensemble methods compared to homogeneous ensemble method. All used ensemble methods demonstrated similar prediction performance.

References

Aldave, R., Dussault, J.P.: Systematic ensemble learning for regression (2014). arXiv preprint arXiv: 1403.7267

Boetticher, G.: The PROMISE repository of empirical software engineering data. http://promisedata. org/repository (2007)

Brown, G.: Diversity in neural network ensembles. Ph.D. thesis, University of Birmingham (2004)

Challagulla, U.V., Bastani, F.B., Yen, I.L.: A unified framework for defect data analysis using the mbr technique. In: Proceeding of 18th IEEE International Conference on Tools with Artificial Intelligence, pp. 39–46 (2006)

Dietterich, T.G.: Ensemble methods in machine learning. International workshop on multiple classifier systems, pp. 1–15. Springer, Berlin, Heidelberg (2000)

Fenton, N.E., Neil, M.: A critique of software defect prediction models. IEEE Trans. Softw. Eng. 25(5), 675–689 (1999)

Geman, S., Bienenstock, E., Doursat, R.: Neural networks and the bias/variance dilemma. Neural Comput. 4(1), 1–58 (1992)

Holmes, G., Donkin A., Witten, I.H.: Weka: a machine learning workbench. In: Proceedings of the 2nd Australian and New Zealand Conference on Intelligent Information Systems, pp. 357–361 (1994)

Jiang, Y., Cukic, B., Ma, Y.: Techniques for evaluating fault prediction models. Empir. Softw. Eng. 13(5), 561–595 (2008)

Khoshgoftaar, T.M., Geleyn, E., Nguyen, L.: Empirical case studies of combining software quality classification models. In: Proceedings of 3rd International Conference on Quality Software, pp. 40–49 (2003)

LeBlanc, M., Tibshirani, R.: Combining estimates in regression and classification. J. Am. Stat. Assoc. 91(436), 1641–1650 (1996)

Lessmann, S., Baesens, B., Mues, C., Pietsch, S.: Benchmarking classification models for software defect prediction: a proposed framework and novel findings. IEEE Trans. Softw. Eng. 34(4), 485–496 (2008)

Mendes-Moreira, J., Soares, C., Jorge, A.M., Sousa, J.F.D.: Ensemble approaches for regression: a survey. ACM Comput. Surv. (CSUR) 45(1), 1–40 (2012)

Menzies, T., Milton, Z., Turhan, B., Cukic, B., Jiang, Y., Bener, A.: Defect prediction from static code features: current results, limitations, new approaches. Autom. Softw. Eng. 17(4), 375–407 (2010)

Merz, C.J.: Classification and regression by combining models. Ph.D. thesis, University of California, Irvine (1998)

Podgurski, A., Yang, C.: Partition testing, stratified sampling, and cluster analysis. Proc. ACM SIGSOFT Softw. Eng. Notes 18, 169–181 (1993)

Rathore, S.S., Kumar, S.: Linear and non-linear heterogeneous ensemble methods to predict the number of faults in software systems. Knowl. Based Syst. **119**, 232–256 (2017)

Sun, Z., Song, Q., Zhu, X.: Using coding-based ensemble learning to improve software defect prediction. IEEE Trans. Syst. Man Cybern. Part C Appl. Rev. **42**(6), 1806–1817 (2012)

Vandecruys, O., Martens, D., Baesens, B., Mues, C., De Backer, M., Haesen, R.: Mining software repositories for comprehensible software fault prediction models. J. Syst. Softw. **81**(5), 823–839 (2008)

Wang, T., Zhang, Z., Jing, X., Zhang, L.: Multiple kernel ensemble learning for software defect prediction. Autom. Softw. Eng., 1–22 (2015)

Chapter 5
Nonlinear Rule Based Ensemble Methods for the Prediction of Number of Faults

In the previous chapter, we explored the use of linear rule based ensemble methods for the number of faults prediction. In that work, we used four different ensemble methods, each of them combines the outputs of base learners in a linear form. Results of experimental analysis showed that a stable and accurate fault prediction performance could be achieved using linear rule based ensemble methods. However, these ensemble methods capture only the weighted contributions of base learners and combine them in linear way, which may sometimes suffer from the linearity error problem of fitting in a straight line [1].

Another way to build the ensemble methods is to combine the output of base learners in a nonlinear way. In this type of ensemble methods, generally a nonlinear learning technique is used to combine the outputs of base learners for the ensemble. By using a nonlinear technique for ensemble combination, we can capture contribution/influence of base learners in a way that is more precise. The prediction models based on this type of ensembles provide better, accurate, and stable fault prediction performance.

5.1 Nonlinear Rule Based Heterogeneous Ensemble Methods

In this type of ensemble methods, more than one learning techniques are used to generate base learners for the ensemble. The base learner generation process is same as followed for the linear rule based ensemble methods. The difference lies in the way outputs of base learners combined for the ensemble. In these ensemble methods, a nonlinear learning technique is used to combine the outputs [2]. This technique forms a nonlinear relationship between input values and output values input to it. Outputs of each base learning technique in the form of predicted number

© The Author(s), under exclusive license to Springer Nature Singapore Pte Ltd. 2019   59
S. S. Rathore and S. Kumar, *Fault Prediction Modeling for the Prediction*
of Number of Software Faults, SpringerBriefs in Computer Science,
https://doi.org/10.1007/978-981-13-7131-8_5

of faults for the validation dataset is treated as input values and outputs of each base learning technique in the form of predicted number of faults for testing dataset is treated as output values. A nonlinear learning technique trains for the input values and produces a final output, which is a nonlinear combination of output values [3, 4].

5.2   Evaluation of Nonlinear Rule Based Heterogeneous Ensemble Methods

The evaluation of nonlinear rule based ensemble methods is performed via an experimental analysis for various open-source software fault datasets. The elements of experimental analysis such as experimental procedure, software fault dataset, tools used, etc., are described in the upcoming subsections.

5.2.1   Software Fault Datasets

The used software fault datasets are accumulated from the PROMISE data repository to build and evaluate heterogeneous ensemble methods base fault prediction models [5]. We have used same 28 software fault datasets as described in Chap. 3 of Sect. 3.2.1. All the used fault datasets have same 20 object-oriented software metrics (independent variables) and number of faults information as dependent variable. A Detailed description of these datasets is given in Chap. 3.

5.2.2   Experimental Setup

As described in Chap. 3, we have categorized used software fault datasets into four different groups based on the percentage of faulty modules in given fault datasets. Subsequently, we built and evaluated prediction models for each group of fault datasets. Details about different groups of software fault datasets are given in Table 3.2. Group-1 contains all the fault datasets having percentage of faulty software modules below 10%. Fault datasets have faulty software modules between 10 and 20% categorized into group-2. Fault datasets have faulty software modules between 20 and 30% categorized into group-3. Group-4 contains all the fault datasets have 30% or more faulty software modules.

5.2.3   Experimental Procedure

The experimental procedure adopted for building and evaluating nonlinear hetero-geneous ensemble methods based fault prediction models is given in Table 5.1. The experimental procedure is adopted from the work presented by [2].

The following steps describe working of nonlinear rule based ensemble method.

Table 5.1 Experimental procedure for non-linear rule based heterogeneous ensemble methods

Input: D: A set of twenty-eight software fault dataset augmented with object-oriented software metrics and fault information, D= $\{D_1, D_2, ..., D_{28}\}$
S: A set of L base learning techniques S= $s_1,...,s_L,$//Here, Base learning techniques ={ Linear regression, Multilayer perceptron, Decision tree regression}
Preprocessing:
Split the whole fault dataset into three parts as training dataset, validation dataset, and testing dataset.
Training dataset TR = $tr_1,...,tr_N$ containing N modules
Validation dataset V = $v_1,...,v_V$ containing V modules
Testing dataset TE = $te_1,...,te_R$ containing R modules
Begin:
1. for each learning techniques $s_j \in S, j = 1,...,L$
2.   Train s_j over TR
3. end for
4. for each module in validation dataset $v_i \epsilon V, i=1,...,V$
5.   for each learning techniques $s_j \in S, j = 1,...,L$
6.   Apply learning technique s_j over v_i
7.   Calculate the estimated the number of faults E_f
8.   Store E_f
9.   end for
10. end for
11. Store actual values of faults in each v_j in a vector Y

(continued)

Table 5.1 (continued)

12. Store the estimated number of faults (E_f) of each $s_j \in S$ in a data matrix (E), such that E= $\{E_f^1, E_f^2, \ldots, E_f^L, Y\}$

13. Train a model (X) over E, where, X is a non-linear learning technique

14. for each e $\in$ E

15. Apply the trained model X over E

16.   Final Prediction = the prediction made by X over E

    end for

End

Partition the fault dataset: We partitioned original fault dataset into three disjoint subsets as training dataset (60% of original dataset), validation dataset (20% of original dataset), and testing dataset (20% of original dataset). The dataset partitions are generated by using stratification process, in which total population is partitioned into nonoverlapping partitions. Each partition receives proper representation of the population distribution [6]. The advantage of using stratification process is that it keeps the data distribution in each partition close to that in the entire population.

Training of learning technique for base learners generation: To generate base learners for the ensemble, each used learning technique, linear regression, decision tree regression, and multilayer perceptron is trained for the training dataset.

Apply each learning technique over the validation dataset: Each trained base learning technique is applied over the validation dataset. The estimated value of number of faults for each validation dataset module is stored in data matrix.

Training of nonlinear model (M): The stored estimated value of number of faults by each learning technique for validation dataset modules is used as independent variables and their corresponding actual value of faults is used as the dependent variable. This dataset is used to train a nonlinear model to model the relationship between input values and output values.

Apply the trained model (X) over the unseen testing modules: The trained base learning techniques are applied over the testing dataset and their predicted number of faults values are stored in a data matrix. This data matrix is served as testing dataset. The trained nonlinear model X is applied to this testing dataset. The final prediction of ensemble method is the output predicted by model (X) [7].

5.2.4 Nonlinear Learning Technique

We have used regression forest and gradient boosting regression as nonlinear techniques for the ensemble methods.

Regression forest technique: Regression forest is a type of random forest technique. However, it is used for the regression task where dependent variable is of continuous type [8]. The underlying functionality of regression forest is same as random forest used for classification. It builds a regression tree initially by selecting the most promising attribute (feature) as the root node and by splitting the data based on the selection of the root node. It continues building tree in this fashion iteratively by selecting promising intermediate nodes and by splitting the data accordingly [9]. Standard Deviation metric is generally used to choose the attribute on which the data has split at the node. The attribute with the highest decrease in standard deviation is used as the root node and further intermediate nodes are also chosen based on decrement in standard deviation. Once regression tree is built, next task is how to make the prediction when leaf node is reached. Each leaf node in the tree may contain multiple examples of the training dataset. Typically, average of target variables of leaf node examples is used as the output for test example that follows the path from the root to leaf node [10].

Multiple Additive Regression Trees (MART) technique: Friedman first introduces MART technique in 2001 [11]. It is also known as gradient boosted regression trees. This technique constructs prediction model by following a forward stage-wise additive approach that implemented gradient descent in function space [12]. For ith iteration, the direction of the gradient descent curve is given by the negative gradient of the loss function defined by Eq. 5.1.

$$-g_i(x) = -\left[\frac{\partial L(y, f(x))}{\partial f(x)}\right] f(x) = f^{(i-1)}(x) \tag{5.1}$$

At each iteration, a regression tree model is fitted to predict the negative gradient. This technique also uses shrinkage, where the step length at each iteration is multiplied by some factor α $(0 < \alpha <= 1)$. It helps in enhancing the model performance in practice. α is also referred as the learning rate, as lowering it will slow down the learning process [13]. Combining all of these, the "step" taken at each iteration i is give by Eq. 5.2.

$$f_i(x) = \alpha \rho_i \theta_i(x). \tag{5.2}$$

where the step length ρ_i can be different for each region.

5.2.5   Tools and Techniques Used for Experiment

We have used *RemovePercentage* filter to partition the original fault dataset into training dataset, validation dataset, and testing dataset. The implementation of this filter is available in the Weka machine learning tool. Further, Weka implementation of base learning techniques is used for base learner generations used in ensemble methods [14]. To assess the performance of built fault prediction models, we have used mean absolute error (MAE), mean relative error (MRE), and pre (0.30) performance measures.

5.3 Results and Discussion

As per the experimental procedure described in Table 5.1, we have built nonlinear rule based ensemble methods for the prediction of number of faults in software systems. All used fault datasets have been categorized into four different groups as identified in Table 3.2. We reported results in terms of mean absolute error (MAE) and mean relative error (MRE), and pred(0.30). Tables 5.2, 5.3, 5.4, and 5.5 show results of experimental analysis for MAE and MRE performance measures. Each table is corresponding to one group of software fault datasets. For each performance measure, we have reported summarized results in terms of minimum, average, and maximum value of each ensemble method.

5.3.1 Results of Group-1 for MAE and MRE

Table 5.2 shows the results in terms of MAE and MRE for five group-1 fault datasets have less than 10% faulty software modules. The observations based on Table 5.2 are summarized below.

Table 5.2 Results of experiment for group-1 datasets (Datasets have less than 10% of faulty modules, 5 datasets)

Technique	MAE			MRE		
	Min	Avg.	Max	Min	Avg.	Max
Regression forest (RF) ensemble method	0.058	0.104	0.157	0.029	0.042	0.057
Multiple additive regression trees (MART) ensemble method	0.058	0.104	0.1623	0.029	0.049	0.079

Table 5.3 Results of experiment for group-2 datasets (Datasets have faulty modules between 10 and 20%, 12 datasets)

Technique	MAE			MRE		
	Min	Avg.	Max	Min	Avg.	Max
Regression forest (RF) ensemble method	0.1552	0.366	0.7912	0.0612	0.210	0.56
Multiple additive regression trees (MART) ensemble method	0.0952	0.344	0.974	0.0423	0.189	0.620

Table 5.4 Results of experiment for group-3 datasets (Datasets have faulty modules between 20 and 30%, 3 datasets)

Technique	MAE			MRE		
	Min	Avg.	Max	Min	Avg.	Max
Regression forest (RF) ensemble method	0.362	0.554	0.672	0.236	0.262	0.310
Multiple additive regression trees (MART) ensemble method	0.315	0.573	0.737	0.198	0.266	0.374

Table 5.5 Results of experiment for group-4 datasets (Datasets have 30% or more faulty modules, 8 datasets)

Technique	MAE			MRE		
	Min	Avg.	Max	Min	Avg.	Max
Regression forest (RF) ensemble method	0.269	0.899	1.86	0.0904	0.404	0.98
Multiple additive regression trees (MART) ensemble method	0.252	0.885	1.79	0.0871	0.423	1.03

- With respect to the MAE measure, RF ensemble method produced minimum error value of 0.05, average error value of 0.104, and maximum value 0.157. MART ensemble method produced minimum error value of 0.058, average value of 0.104, and maximum error value of 0.162. The best performance is produced by RF ensemble method.
- With respect to the MRE measure, RF ensemble method produced minimum error value of 0.029, average error value of 0.042, and maximum value 0.057. MART ensemble method produced minimum error value of 0.029, average value of 0.104, and maximum value of 0.079. Again, the best performance is produced by RF ensemble method.
- Overall, both ensemble methods produced same minimum and average values but RF ensemble method produced lower maximum value and outperformed MART ensemble method.

5.3.2 Results of Group-2 for MAE and MRE

Table 5.3 shows the results in terms of MAE and MRE for twelve group-2 fault datasets having faulty software module between 10 and 20%. The observations based on Table 5.3 are summarized below.

- For MAE measure, RF ensemble method produced minimum error value of 0.1552, average error value of 0.36, and maximum value 0.791. MART ensemble method produced minimum error value of 0.09, average value of 0.344, and maximum error value of 0.97. The best performance is produced by MART ensemble method, except for maximum value.

- For MRE measure, RF ensemble method produced minimum error value of 0.061, average error value of 0.21, and maximum value 0.56. MART ensemble method produced minimum error value of 0.042, average value of 0.189, and maximum error value of 0.62. Again, best performance is produced by MART ensemble method, except for maximum value.
- Overall, MART ensemble method produced lower minimum and average values but RF ensemble method produced lower maximum value.

5.3.3 Results of Group-3 for MAE and MRE

Table 5.4 shows the results in terms of MAE and MRE for three group-3 fault datasets have faulty software modules between 20 and 30%. The observations based on Table 5.4 are summarized below.

- In terms of MAE measure, RF ensemble method produced minimum error value of 0.36, average error value of 0.554 and maximum value 0.672. MART ensemble method produced minimum error value of 0.315, average value of 0.573, and maximum error value of 0.737. The best performance is produced by RF ensemble method except for minimum error value.
- In terms of MRE measure, RF ensemble method produced minimum error value of 0.236, average error value of 0.262, and maximum value 0.310. MART ensemble method produced minimum error value of 0.198, average value of 0.266, and maximum error value of 0.374. Again, the best performance is produced by RF ensemble method except for minimum error value.
- Overall, RF ensemble methods produced better performance as compared to MART ensemble method except for minimum error value.

5.3.4 Results of Group-4 for MAE and MRE

Group-4 included fault datasets have faulty software modules 30% or more. Eight fault datasets have been fallen into this group. Summarized results for this group in terms of MAE and MRE are given in Table 5.5. The observations based on the table are summarized below.

- With respect to the MAE measure, RF ensemble method produced minimum error value of 0.26, average error value of 0.89, and maximum value 1.86. MART ensemble method produced minimum error value of 0.25, average value of 0.88, and maximum error value of 1.79. The best performance is produced by MART ensemble method.
- With respect to the MRE measure, RF ensemble method produced minimum error value of 0.09, average error value of 0.40, and maximum value 0.98. MART ensemble method produced minimum error value of 0.08, average value of 0.42, and maximum error value of 1.03. Again, RF ensemble method produced relatively better performance.

- Overall, RF ensemble methods produced better performance as compared to MART ensemble method except for minimum error value.

From the results, it has been observed that generally, both ensemble methods produced better performance, when number of faulty modules in software systems are low (below 30%). As percentage of faulty modules increase, performance of ensemble methods decreases. This trend has been followed by both used ensemble methods. However, low variation among the performance of used ensemble methods has been found. It shows more stable performance of heterogeneous ensemble methods with compared to homogeneous ensemble method.

5.3.5   Results of Pred(0.30) for All Groups of Fault Datasets

Tables 5.6, 5.7, 5.8, and 5.9 show results of pred(0.30) performance measure for both nonlinear rule based heterogeneous ensemble methods. The results are summarized in terms of minimum, median, and maximum of one group of datasets in each table. The following observations have been drawn from these tables as discussed below.

- For group-1 fault datasets, RF ensemble method produced minimum value of 89.7%, median value of 91.7%, and maximum value of 95.6%. Similarly, MART ensemble method produced minimum value of 88.3%, median value of 91.7% and

Table 5.6 Pred(0.30) results of experiment for group-1 datasets

Technique	Pred(0.30)		
	Min (%)	Median (%)	Max (%)
Regression forest (RF) ensemble method	89.70	91.70	95.60
Multiple additive regression trees (MART) ensemble method	88.30	91.70	95.60

Table 5.7 Pred(0.30) results of experiment for group-2 datasets

Technique	Pred(0.30)		
	Min (%)	Median (%)	Max (%)
Regression forest (RF) ensemble method	59.00	83.50	92.90
Multiple additive regression trees (MART) ensemble method	64.30	79.90	92.00

Table 5.8 Pred(0.30) results of experiment for group-3 datasets

Technique	Pred(0.30)		
	Min (%)	Median (%)	Max (%)
Regression forest (RF) ensemble method	66.70	72.40	73.70
Multiple additive regression trees (MART) ensemble method	70.40	71.40	75.80

Table 5.9 Pred(0.30) results of experiment for group-4 datasets

Technique	Pred(0.30)		
	Min (%)	Median (%)	Max (%)
Regression forest (RF) ensemble method	26.40	49.30	80.7%
Multiple additive regression trees (MART) ensemble method	22.06	54.90	81.30

maximum value of 95.6%. Both ensemble methods performed similarly except for minimum value, where RF ensemble method performed better.

- For group-2 fault datasets, RF ensemble method produced minimum value of 59.0%, median value of 83.5%, and maximum value of 92.9%. Similarly, MART ensemble method produced minimum value of 64.3%, median value of 79.9%, and maximum value of 92.0%. RF ensemble method performed better compared to MART ensemble method except for minimum value, where MART ensemble method performed better.
- With respect to group-3 fault datasets, RF ensemble method produced minimum value of 66.7%, median value of 72.4%, and maximum value of 73.7%. Similarly, MART ensemble method produced minimum value of 70.4%, median value of 71.4%, and maximum value of 75.8%. MART ensemble method performed better compared to RF ensemble method except for median value, where RF ensemble method performed better.
- For group-4 fault datasets, RF ensemble method produced minimum value of 26.4%, median value of 49.3%, and maximum value of 80.7%. Similarly, MART ensemble method produced minimum value of 22.06%, median value of 54.9%, and maximum value of 81.3%. MART ensemble method performed better compared to RF ensemble method except for minimum value, where RF ensemble method performed better.
- Overall, it has found that MART ensemble method performed better compared to RF ensemble method for most of the cases.

5.4 Summary

This chapter presented an evaluation of two nonlinear rule based heterogeneous ensemble methods for the prediction of number of faults. Ensemble methods were built by combining the prediction outputs of multiple learning techniques (base learners) in nonlinear form with the aim to improve the overall performance of fault prediction. The presented experimental study was performed for 28 software fault datasets garnered from the PROMISE data repository and MAE, MRE, and pred(0.30) performance evaluation measures were used to evaluate the performance of ensemble methods. From results, it has been observed that generally, nonlinear rule based heterogeneous ensemble methods produced significant performance, when the number of faulty modules in software systems is low (below 30%). Performance of used ensemble methods slashed marginally for software projects has a higher percentage of faulty modules. A low variation among the performance of used ensemble methods has been found in comparison to used homogeneous ensemble methods. All used ensemble methods demonstrated similar prediction performance.

References

1. Fox, J.: Regression Diagnostics: An Introduction, vol. 79. Sage (1991)
2. Rathore, S.S., Kumar, S.: Linear and non-linear heterogeneous ensemble methods to predict the number of faults in software systems. Knowl.-Based Syst. **119**, 232–256 (2017)
3. Todorovski, L., Dzeroski, S.: Combining classifiers with meta decision trees. Mach. Learn. **50**(3), 223–249 (2003)
4. Webb, G.I., Zheng, Z.: Multistrategy ensemble learning: Reducing error by combining ensemble learning techniques. IEEE Trans. Knowl. Data Eng. **16**(8), 980–991 (2004)
5. Boetticher, G.: The PROMISE repository of empirical software engineering data (2007). http://promisedata.org/repository
6. Agrawal, R., Srikant, R.: Privacy-preserving data mining. ACM **29**(2), 439–450 (2000)
7. Breiman, L.: Stacked regressions. Mach. Learn. **24**(1), 49–64 (1996)
8. Fiaschi, L., Köthe, U., Nair, R., Hamprecht, F.A.: Learning to count with regression forest and structured labels. In: Proceedings of 21st International Conference on Pattern Recognition (ICPR), pp. 2685–2688 (2012)
9. Criminisi, A., Shotton, J., Konukoglu, E.: Decision forests: A unified framework for classification, regression, density estimation, manifold learning and semi-supervised learning. Found. Trends Comput. Graph. Vis. **7**(2–3), 81–227 (2012)
10. Liaw, A., Wiener, M.: Classification and regression by random forest. R News **2**(3), 18–22 (2002)
11. Friedman, J.H., Meulman, J.J.: Multiple additive regression trees with application in epidemiology. Stat. Med. **22**(9), 1365–1381 (2003)
12. Elish, M.O.: Improved estimation of software project effort using multiple additive regression trees. Expert Syst. Appl. **36**(7), 10774–10778 (2009)
13. Stone, C.J.: Additive regression and other nonparametric models. Ann. Stat. 689–705 (1985)
14. Witten, I.H., Frank E., Hall, M.A., Pal, C.J.: Data Mining: Practical Machine Learning Tools and Techniques. Morgan Kaufmann

Chapter 6
Conclusions

This chapter concludes the book. The book primarily aimed to present fault prediction modeling for the prediction of number of faults in software systems. It covered details of regression and ensemble methods used for the prediction of number of faults. Further, evaluation of different homogeneous and heterogeneous ensemble methods was presented. The work presented in this book could be advantageous to the new researchers and software practitioners in terms of selecting the appropriate technique/methods when predicting number of faults.

Chapter 1 introduced basic concepts of the software fault prediction. Further, it discussed basic terminologies of software fault prediction, classification of software faults/bugs, and benefits of software fault prediction in the software quality assurance process. Additionally, chapter listed out contributions of the presented work. In the end, chapter summarized organization of the book.

Chapter 2 discussed various regression techniques used earlier for the prediction of number of faults in software systems. Further, it described different ensemble methods for the regression. State-of-the-art about the techniques used for the prediction of number of faults was also presented in the chapter. At the end chapter presented different performance measures used for the evaluation of built fault prediction models.

Chapter 3 presented an evaluation of five homogeneous ensemble methods for the number of faults prediction. Some of the used ensemble methods already evaluated for software fault prediction and some other ensemble methods are novel in the presented study. A total 15 fault prediction models have built for each fault dataset. The experimental analysis was performed for 28 software fault datasets grouped into four different groups based on the percentage of faulty modules in the datasets. Experimental results showed that used homogeneous ensemble methods produced a better performance when a number of faulty modules in software systems is low (below 20%). As the percentage of faulty modules increases, the performance of ensemble methods decreases. Overall, rotation forest, bagging, and random subspace

© The Author(s), under exclusive license to Springer Nature Singapore Pte Ltd. 2019
S. S. Rathore and S. Kumar, *Fault Prediction Modeling for the Prediction
of Number of Software Faults*, SpringerBriefs in Computer Science,
https://doi.org/10.1007/978-981-13-7131-8_6

occupied the top three positions and performed better as compared to other used ensemble methods. Decision tree regression as base learner outperformed other used base learning techniques.

Chapter 4 focused on the evaluation of linear rule based heterogeneous ensemble methods for the prediction of number of faults. Presented ensemble methods utilized the capabilities of multiple learning techniques and combined them in a linear form to improve the overall performance of fault prediction. Presented study explored the use of four different linear rule based ensemble methods and evaluated the performance of used methods through an experimental analysis for 28 software fault datasets. Results showed that generally, linear rule based heterogeneous ensemble methods produced better performance, when number of faulty modules in software systems are low (below 20%). This trend has been followed by most of the used ensemble methods. Moreover, a low variation among the performance of used ensemble methods has been found. It shows more stable performance of heterogeneous ensemble methods in comparison to homogeneous ensemble method. All used ensemble methods demonstrated similar prediction performance.

Chapter 5 presented an evaluation of two nonlinear rule based heterogeneous ensemble methods for the prediction of number of faults. Ensemble methods were built by combining the prediction outputs of multiple learning techniques (base learners) in nonlinear form. The presented study was performed for 28 software fault datasets garnered from the PROMISE data repository and MAE, MRE, and pred(0.30) performance evaluation measures were used to evaluate the performance of ensemble methods. It has been observed that generally, nonlinear rule based heterogeneous ensemble methods produced significant performance, when the number of faulty modules in software systems is low (below 30%). Performance of used ensemble methods slashed marginally for software projects has a higher percentage of faulty modules. A low variation among the performance of used ensemble methods has been found in comparison to used homogeneous ensemble methods.

When we compared the overall performance of ensemble methods including homogeneous and heterogeneous ensemble methods, following specific conclusions have been drawn from experimental studies as discussed below.

- Among the used homogeneous ensemble methods overall, bagging, rotation forest, and random subspace performed better compared to other used ensemble methods. However, a high variation in the performance of homogeneous ensemble methods has been noticed for different used fault datasets.
- When comparing results of used homogeneous ensemble method with linear rule based heterogeneous ensemble methods, it has been found that earlier ensemble methods produced average MAE value in the range of 0.09–0.80 and minimum MRE value in the range of 0.05–0.52. In the case of later ensemble methods, average MAE value is in the range of 0.10–0.90 and minimum MRE value is in the range of 0.04–0.55. For pred(0.30) measure, earlier ensemble methods produced median value in the range of 39.8–89.8%, and later ensemble methods produced value in the range of 49.3–91.8%. Both types of ensemble methods performed

similarly for MAE and MRE performance measures but for pred(0.30) measure later ones outperformed earlier ensemble methods.

- When comparing the results of homogeneous ensemble methods with nonlinear rule based heterogeneous ensemble methods, it has been observed that later ones produced average MAE value in the range of 0.05–0.88 and minimum MRE value in the range of 0.04–0.42. For pred(0.30) measure, later ones ensemble methods produced median value in the range of 49.3–91.7%. These results showed that nonlinear heterogeneous ensemble methods produced relatively better results as compared to homogeneous ensemble methods for the used performance measures.
- When comparing the results of linear rule based heterogeneous with nonlinear rule based heterogeneous ensemble methods, it has been observed that both types of methods performed similarly, however, later ones performed marginally better as compared to the earlier ensemble methods.

Based on these observations, we suggest to use heterogeneous ensemble method specially, nonlinear rule based to build the fault prediction models for the prediction of number of faults in the software system. One of the main advantages of heterogeneous ensemble method s is that they use diverse base learners, which may be helpful in the overall improvement of the prediction results.

Closing Remarks

This book covers the basics as well as summarizes the research works reported in the literature in the area of software fault prediction especially for the prediction of number of faults. The main objective of the book is to summarize the publicly available information in the area of prediction of number of software faults. Along with the summary of works, the book provides easy pointers to the corresponding detailed documents. The book also includes the summary of various published works by the authors and their other team members who have worked with them previously. In this book, initially the basic topics on software fault prediction are discussed. Then, discussion on the number of software fault prediction especially the use of ensemble methods is provided. The book provides a good coverage on the linear rule based and non-linear rule based ensemble methods along with the corresponding experimentations for the prediction of number of software faults. So, the book can be useful to not only the beginners but also provide some fruitful ideas to the trained researchers in this domain. We expect that the readers will like the book and will find it easy to understand. The experimental studies presented in the book can also be really helpful to the readers. To better understand the results, various table and figures have been provided. We are hopeful that it will provide better reading experience to the readers.

© The Author(s), under exclusive license to Springer Nature Singapore Pte Ltd. 2019   75
S. S. Rathore and S. Kumar, *Fault Prediction Modeling for the Prediction
of Number of Software Faults*, SpringerBriefs in Computer Science,
https://doi.org/10.1007/978-981-13-7131-8

Index

© The Author(s), under exclusive license to Springer Nature Singapore Pte Ltd. 2019   77
S. S. Rathore and S. Kumar, *Fault Prediction Modeling for the Prediction
of Number of Software Faults*, SpringerBriefs in Computer Science,
https://doi.org/10.1007/978-981-13-7131-8